This Dream Is Not for You

This Dream Is Not for You

Learn to Live by Letting Go

WADE JOYE

Nashville • New York

Worthy
Hachette Book Group
1290 Avenue of the Americas, New York, NY 10104
worthypublishing.com
twitter.com/worthypub

First Edition: September 2023

Worthy is a division of Hachette Book Group, Inc. The Worthy name and logo are trademarks of Hachette Book Group, Inc.

The publisher is not responsible for websites (or their content) that are not owned by the publisher.

The Hachette Speakers Bureau provides a wide range of authors for speaking events. To find out more, go to hachettespeakersbureau.com or email HachetteSpeakers@hbgusa.com.

Worthy Books may be purchased in bulk for business, educational, or promotional use. For information, please contact your local bookseller or the Hachette Book Group Special Markets Department at special.markets@hbgusa.com.

Print book interior design by Bart Dawson.

Library of Congress Cataloging-in-Publication Data has been applied for.

ISBNs: 978-1-5460-0479-0 (hardcover); 978-1-5460-0481-3 (ebook)

Printed in the United States of America

LSC-C

Printing 1, 2023

To my mom and dad, the first ones to fan the flame of my dreams, and who still do so to this day.

And to Ferris, Liana, Adleigh, and Sydney—you are my dreams now become reality, and daily exceed what I could have ever hoped for or imagined. Thank you for filling my life with joy and laughter. I love you always and forever, no matter what.

Contents

Foreword, by Carlos Whittaker ix

Introduction. "What Should I Dream About?" 1

Part I. Redefine Your Dream

Chapter 1. The Day My Dream Died 11

Chapter 2. The Dangers in Your Dream 23

Chapter 3. The Striving Self vs.
the Surrendered Self 37

Part II. Release Your Grip

Chapter 4. Dream with Open Hands 53

Chapter 5. Upgrade Your Disappointment 77

Chapter 6. Face the Facts. 95

Part III. Reclaim Your Purpose

Chapter 7. Notice Your Narrative 123

Chapter 8. The Calling to Consistency 147

Part IV. Run Your Race

Chapter 9. Don't Give Up on Your Race 173

Chapter 10. Guard Your Gratitude 193

Conclusion. Reawaken Your Expectation
and Keep Dreaming 213

Acknowledgments 223

About the Author. 229

by Carlos Whittaker

When I was a kid in 1986—just imagine any of the *Stranger Things* kids (that was me)—I would have this reoccurring dream. I was standing on the top of a hill with green grass and with bright blue skies above me. I held a sword in both hands and my feet were planted firmly in the ground beneath me. I was staring fiercely at an army of dragons that were charging toward me. The second they got to me I slayed them all with the grace and fluidity of Luke Skywalker with Yoda on his back. And I would always wake up feeling refreshed and victorious; ready to slay whatever dragons the fourth grade had for me that day.

And then I grew up.

My dreams turned from slaying dragons to running from dragons. Running away from things instead of running towards things. And then as I got even older, my dreaming actually stopped. Like I would wake up and not remember a thing I dreamt the night before. That's because I was actually scared to dream. I was scared to dream while I was awake, and scared to dream while I was asleep. It seemed that all my dreams had gone from victorious to defeating.

And because I had stopped dreaming, I had actually stopped living. I was making choices in life that were destroying my dreams left and right. I was sabotaging my dreams, because I could no longer stand the disappointment of not reaching them.

Enter Wade Joye.

In 2011, I had sabotaged what I thought was the last of my dreams. The dream of a happy family. I texted Wade and let him know that I could no longer lead worship at Elevation because I was no longer living with my family… Wade probably doesn't remember this but he texted back… "God is going to do great things through you Carlos. I can't wait to watch."

And can I tell you something…

The first person to invite me back into my dream of leading worship after healing was accomplished was Wade. I stood on the Elevation Church stage on Easter Sunday of 2011 with my family in front of me and my dreams resuscitated back to life.

What's funny is I'm no longer a worship leader. I'm now impacting more people in my late forties that I EVER DREAMED I COULD HAVE. And that dream didn't come to pass until I was forty-seven years old.

Wade Joye is a walking example of someone who not only has walked this walk but has breathed dreams into those around him.

This book is about to take you places you never dreamed you could go.

You ready to dream?

Let's go.

"What Should I Dream About?"

"What should I dream about, Daddy?"

This is the question my three daughters ask me every evening when I walk into their room to kiss them good night.

It started on a family movie night one Friday when I thought our girls were ready for a Joye family rite of passage—their first viewing of *Lord of the Rings*. And when the movie started, the evening held the promise of being an incredible success. My daughters were quickly fascinated by the tales of Middle-earth, and even found a resemblance between the hobbits and their very short (but very brave) father. It was a perfect night. Or at least until Gollum showed up.

If you haven't seen the movie, know that for a young child

Gollum is the stuff of nightmares, and once Gollum was joined by Orcs and all manner of scary creatures from the mind of J. R. R. Tolkien, my kids weren't smiling anymore. They were hiding behind their blankets. After stopping the movie, my wife, Ferris, and I went into damage-control mode. We knew that unless we acted fast, a sleepless night for the girls—and for us—was in the near future. But something unexpected happened while we attempted to get our daughters' minds off of their fear and onto something more positive.

My wife gave the girls a simple prompt to dream that night about going to the beach. Gollum doesn't like the beach, and so they would be safe there. And it worked! Not only did they sleep well that night, but the next evening before bed they asked what they should dream about. And then they asked again the next night after that. And before we knew it, a nightly bedtime ritual was born.

"Tonight you are going on an adventure with baby Yoda to search for new Jedi."

"Dream that you have the powers of Spider-Man without the unfortunate trauma of getting bit by a radioactive spider."

"Dream that you can teleport and visit all seven wonders of the world," to which our girls quickly followed up with "What are the seven wonders of the world?" Our response? "That's the beauty of a dream. You can just make it up!"

After I tell them what to dream about, I tuck them in, kiss them good night, and go downstairs to sit on the couch. Many nights there on the couch I reflect on how blessed we are to actually have these moments. For there was once a time when I wondered if I would ever be able to have a conversation with any of my girls at bedtime.

My wife and I have spent months sitting in a hospital waiting room, begging God to heal our daughters. Those angry, scared, and desperate hospital prayers were our attempts to get God's attention as we tried to pick up the pieces of a dream that appeared to be shattered. We had dreamed of a routine pregnancy and delivery, and of bringing healthy babies home from the hospital. But that was a dream we were never able to experience.

Not only were our twins born three months prematurely, with one suffering a massive grade IV brain bleed, but we were also told by the doctors that we might never take either of them home. And if we did, they might never be what we would consider "normal."

Four years later, we sat in the same hospital waiting room, devastated by the news that our third daughter was diagnosed with cystic fibrosis, a terminal genetic condition. And once again, we were picking up the broken pieces of a dream.

I don't tell you this to make you feel sorry for us or our children. The Lord has been so kind and gracious to our family, and all three of our girls are walking miracles, daily reminders of God's faithfulness. But these moments shook my faith to its core. The theology I had believed until then didn't help me understand how to make sense of it all. I had been taught that the Lord would give you the desires of your heart, and that if you sought first the kingdom of God, all would be added to you. But as I looked around that hospital, thinking about our situation and the situations of the other families there, some of whom were navigating even more difficult circumstances, I began to wrestle with a deep sense of unmet expectations. And I didn't have the ability to reconcile our situation with what I had been taught about the goodness of God.

These doubts didn't arise from only my family's health struggles. During this same time, I watched my dreams for my career take a dramatic turn away from what I had wanted since I was a teenager. I watched friends and family members say goodbye unexpectedly to cherished loved ones. As a pastor, I encountered pain and heartbreak every day in the lives of the people in our congregation. Not to mention the impact of the constant news of those across our country and world living in poverty and oppression who never would have imagined their situation in life when they asked as a child, "What should I dream about?" Maybe they didn't use those same words, but we all have offered up those sentiments to God whether we knew we were praying them or not.

I grew up in the church, part of a family of pastors and ministry leaders. When I was young, I asked God to give me big dreams to accomplish for him one day. And I assumed the dreams that arose in my heart were God's answers to those prayers. My dreams became inextricably linked to what I thought was my calling from God. I was sure these dreams of happiness, fame, impact, and success must be his purpose for my life because they had been birthed in my heart.

I imagine I'm not alone. You may have come to God with

some version of the question "What should I dream about?" And it seems that he filled your heart with a dream. It's human to be a dreamer. We are built to imagine what is not, what could be, and then work to bring that preferred reality to life. In fact, it's part of our mandate from our Creator.

But if we are created by God to dream and experience the fullness of life he promises in Christ, then how do we make sense of the dreams that are in our hearts but always just out of reach? Why would we dream those dreams?

The issue is even more complex. I have met many people—and have been one myself—who have been lucky or blessed enough to actually live their dreams. Maybe that's you, and you are living the dream you prayed for and worked tirelessly to achieve. But as I've learned, many who achieve their dreams often find that the reality of the experience still doesn't live up to the expectation. Something is missing. (And for those of you who are living your dreams today and have found a measure of true happiness, I suspect that someday you'll want more.)

That's because your dream loves to lie to you. Mine lied to me. And not just the selfish dreams either. The good ones lie too. The dreams of career success, ministry influence, or having a family.

I thought that my dream defined me, that it was my purpose, and that fulfilling it was the only way I could bring meaning to my life and find true happiness. My dreams told me that God would never say no to a dream that would honor him.

As I examine my life and the lives of those around me and those throughout history who have followed Jesus, I see something different and unexpectedly beautiful: Jesus is often closest to us within our disappointments. He does some of his best work in the space left by our unmet expectations. I have seen God use a dead dream in my life, and the lives of others, to move us into new seasons of impact and fulfillment that might never have happened if we had stayed on the shores of our own limited imaginations. There was something bigger calling us out beyond what we knew, and often it took the pain of what didn't happen in life to open us up to the possibilities of what could.

This begs the question: What if one of the greatest gifts God could give me was saying no to my dream, even a dream I thought was from him? What if by withholding my dream God was actually leading me to something better?

Throughout my life I have wrestled with questions like these and with what it means to be a dreamer and a Christian, and time and again I'm led back to a question that doesn't even seem to be related to my dreams. It's a deeper question and, ultimately, a much better one: What does it mean to be a disciple?

Only by answering this can we truly understand how to trust God with the dreams in our hearts, and how to embrace the dreams he has for us and the world.

If you're a dreamer, I invite you to join me in asking, What does it mean to be a disciple? If you do, and even if you have been disappointed and are scared to dream again, you will find that Jesus is trustworthy and good, and that even within our greatest defeats, there lie the seeds to something even more exciting and wonderful—resurrection and new life.

I want us to embark on a journey together to find out what it looks like to be disciples *and* dreamers. You don't have to choose one or the other. A disciple of Jesus can be an unashamed dreamer, because the dream for their life has first been released, allowed to fall to the ground and die. Yes, die.

Remember these words of Jesus from John 12:23–25:

> The hour has come for the Son of Man to be glorified. Very truly I tell you, unless a kernel of wheat falls to the ground and dies, it remains only a single seed. But if it dies, it produces many seeds. Anyone who loves their life will lose it, while anyone who hates their life in this world will keep it for eternal life.

Here's the good news of the gospel of Jesus: In the kingdom of God, death is followed by resurrection. You may think that letting your dream die is giving up on your dream, or you may think that your dream has died already, but you have no idea how God is going to multiply what you have entrusted to his hands.

This isn't a call to live passive lives in the name of trust. That's the beauty of walking with Jesus. When we give up control, we can actually live life the way it was meant to be lived.

So how do we realistically get our hearts, emotions, and lives to a place where we are willing to surrender the dreams that are so precious to us?

This book guides you through four basic steps to surrendering and truly living:

- Redefine your dream.
- Release your grip.
- Reclaim your purpose.
- Run your race.

It's only when you have your hands open in the posture of release as a disciple that your heart is finally open to receive what God desires for you. It's your surrender as a disciple that puts you in position to dream the right dreams.

So let's start dreaming together.

PART I

Redefine
Your Dream

CHAPTER 1

The Day My Dream Died

I remember the day my dream died.

It wasn't a dramatic death, or even all that unexpected really. Nothing about the way the day started seemed to indicate a death was imminent. I said goodbye to my wife and three daughters that Tuesday morning like any other day. I drove the same route to Elevation Church headquarters at our Matthews campus in Charlotte, North Carolina, I had taken for years, and I sat through the same weekly worship experience meeting that I did every Tuesday. I thought the meeting went pretty well, but as everyone was leaving something happened that was not on my agenda for the day. It was a conversation I had seen coming for years but always thought was further down the road. I had hoped that if I kept getting better at what I did, maybe the conversation wouldn't come at all. But it did come, and after just one brief conversation and a whisper from God in my soul, I knew it was over.

"This dream is not for you."

I drove home in a daze, bypassed my family as I walked in the door, and went upstairs to my room. As I sat at the foot of my bed, I knew there was no denying the day's ramifications for my life. Because deep in my heart I understood that the conversation I'd had with the leadership of my church was going to mark the end of a season. A season that I'd spent twenty years building, and a season during which I had finally started to see prayers that I prayed for many years answered. But now I began to realize I wasn't going to play the part I had always envisioned. I still had my job as worship pastor so there was a part for me to play, just not the one I had hoped for and, to be honest, not the one I thought God had prepared me for.

"This dream is not for you" are words all of us have heard at one point or another in life. Depending on the circumstances, these words may not even be that unexpected or unfortunate to hear. For example, when I was in the eleventh grade, deep down I knew that my dream of being in a band that toured with Nirvana was most likely not going to happen. And after seeing the tragic way that Nirvana ended, even my teenage heart could understand why I was better off not living that dream.

But what do you do when you hear those six words, "This dream is not for you," and they deny you the real dream you have for your life? The dream to be a husband or a father. A wife or a mother. An artist, a lawyer, a musician, or a business owner? What do you do when you get so close to achieving your dream that you can taste it or almost touch it but still seem destined to live only on the periphery of it? I think this is especially hard in the world we live in, where we are told constantly, both inside and outside the church, that you can achieve anything you put your mind to. Outside the church we are told again and again, "Follow your dreams," and inside the church we hear sermons on Psalm 37:4: "Take delight in the Lord, and he will give you the desires of your heart."

But if the culture says we can do it if we just believe in ourselves enough, and if the Bible says that God will give us our dreams if we just delight in him, then why do we struggle with unrealized dreams? Why do we carry the weight of unfulfilled ambitions?

As I sat on my bed that day, I kept coming back to one question: Why would God give me a dream only to leave it unfulfilled?

THE BIRTH OF A DREAM

For as long as I can remember, I've wanted to be a worship leader and a songwriter. This dream looked different of course over the years. In college I wanted to be the leader of a cool college band, one with the cleverest name. Mine was Gamaliel's Advice. No one could pronounce it or knew what the name meant, so I eventually gave up on cleverness and started the Wade Joye Band. But no matter the name and no matter the music, I came alive when

I led worship. I loved watching people encounter the living God, and the joy of witnessing a song that I had written become the words on the lips of those praising God was like nothing I had ever felt before.

Now granted, none of this happened in packed arenas or sold-out shows. In those days, most of my ministry consisted of youth camps and retreats of thirty or so fifteen-year-olds. I showed up in my baggy khaki pants and braided belt, played my black Gibson Les Paul, and left a sweaty mess on the floor after my one-hour set. But at these events I loved seeing teenagers and college students experience Jesus through music, and I had no doubt I had discovered his purpose for my life.

It was during this season in my early twenties that I prayed a prayer that became an anchor for my dream: "Lord, let me write a song that people all over the world will sing in worship to you." It was an audacious prayer, especially when you looked at the types of gigs the Wade Joye Band had. Playing a cluster of youth camps in the southeastern United States was a far cry from global success, but the dream was born.

It was at one of those youth camps outside Asheville, North Carolina, where I met a fiery young preacher. I was immediately struck by this young man's preaching gift. He was in his early twenties, yet I had never seen someone preach like that before. He held the attention of teenagers not just with his passion but also with his teaching from God's Word. He preached with an urgency, as if that one sermon meant everything to him and was the last chance for someone in the audience to experience Jesus.

And even though his sermons were for teenagers, through his teaching God turned me inside out every session. What was particularly cool was that at the top of one of his sessions he picked up my guitar and led worship. I may or may not have been a little jealous that he could preach *and* lead worship, but needless to say, I was marked by that week with Pastor Steven Furtick. And little did I know that God was going to use that encounter years later to call me into the amazing journey and privilege of helping bring Pastor Steven's dream to life at Elevation Church.

In 2007 Pastor Steven invited me to be a part of leading and growing what was to become Elevation Worship. His vision was that our church would regularly write songs as monuments to the faithfulness of God, songs that gave our church its own vocabulary of worship. And he also said that one day the world would sing these songs. At that point, Elevation Church was meeting in a high school in Charlotte, yet the words Pastor Steven spoke were authoritative and felt realistic.

The next seven years told a story of miracle after miracle. Thousands of people professed faith in Christ and were baptized as a result of God moving through Elevation Church. New campuses launched both inside and outside Charlotte. Miracles were granted for my family as my premature twins defied expectations and came home as healthy girls after months in the NICU. And then there was the miracle of our third daughter, who was born with cystic fibrosis yet thrived—and thrives today as a healthy girl despite the fear attached to that diagnosis.

I was a part of writing not only songs that chronicled my

journey of doubt, faith, and clinging to God in these seasons but also songs that the Lord used in our church. And while the songs we wrote at the beginning proved the patience and love of our church, who had grace for us as we learned how to write a worship song, we began to see the vision Pastor Steven talked about come to life. The songs also got better as he became involved in the songwriting process. I was blessed to be a part of writing songs with him like "O Come to the Altar." I was able to lead these songs in our church and sing some of them on our albums. God had heard the prayer I prayed years before about being a part of writing songs the world sings, and I was seeing it come to pass before my very eyes. I was living the dream. Leading worship, writing songs, serving as worship pastor for one of the greatest churches in the world. And at home, my family was thriving.

But along the way, Pastor Steven would tell me that he saw something in me for a different ministry. Throughout the years, he would say that he saw me more as a church builder than a worship leader. That my vocal and writing talent was good, but that I had the gifting of a great pastor. He told me that one day I would need to make a choice—be a great leader and church builder, or an average worship leader. I fought that as long as I could. And I made every excuse I could think of. Other people may be better singers, but *I* had an "anointing." It must be God's will for me to lead and write because I love it so much. Why would the Lord let me love something that he didn't want me to do? But deep down I began to realize that what Pastor Steven said was right—there were people coming into our ministry more gifted at leading worship than me, and there were much better songwriters. If I continued to chase the dream of being a worship leader instead of transitioning to a new role, would I be limiting the growth of our ministry?

I didn't want to admit the truth, but I realized that though I was always telling our worship team to submit to a vision that was bigger than them, I was unwilling to surrender the deepest parts of myself.

A FIRST WORLD PITY PARTY

My dream was not going to give up without a fight, though, which is why on the day I was told I would need to eventually step away from my role with Elevation Worship, both in leading worship and songwriting, I was angry. My prayers were not prayers of peace and trust. I was confused, hurt, and seemingly lost.

I came home and told God that this couldn't be what he wanted for me. It had to be a test to see if I was willing to give something up. How could I step away from a dream that gave me so much joy and life, and then watch other people enjoy the fruit of what I had labored to produce? It was a first world pity party. I even felt guilty for feeling disappointed because I knew how much God had given me already. But the emotions were real because the dream was real. I was both living it and also looking forward to all the incredible possibilities of my dream.

"This dream is not for you."

I didn't like hearing that phrase echoing in my mind. So I made my best case before God. I presented my motivations and told him how pure they were, and how my dream was all for his glory. Then I sat there, waiting for God to speak. Waiting for the Lord to tell me I was right and they were wrong. But the vindication never came. As I sat there in silence, hoping for some dramatic word from God in my spirit, I grew desperate for God to speak. It was then that I noticed my Bible sitting on the dresser right in front of me. I hate to admit that it took me so long to see what God's Word had to say, but I got there eventually. I took my Bible, and the bookmark opened right to the following verses:

David summoned all the officials of Israel to assemble at Jerusalem: the officers over the tribes, the commanders of the divisions in the service of the king, the commanders of thousands and commanders of hundreds, and the officials in charge of all the property and livestock belonging to the king and his sons, together with the palace officials, the warriors and all the brave fighting men.

King David rose to his feet and said: "Listen to me, my fellow Israelites, my people. I had it in my heart to build a house as a place of rest for the ark of the covenant of the LORD, for the footstool of our God, and I made plans to build it. But God said to me, 'You are not to build a house for my Name, because you are a warrior and have shed blood.'" (1 Chronicles 28:1–3)

First of all, I don't normally recommend just opening the Bible randomly and taking the first verse you see as a word from God. But in this case, the application was too obvious. While I didn't think of myself as a warrior or could ever recall shedding blood that wasn't my own, the message for me was one of the clearest I had ever heard from God. Here was David, a man who had a dream to glorify God, and God said no: *"This dream is not for you."* David's greatest ambition—to build a house of worship for God—was denied by God and given to someone else. How could that be when David's motives seemed pure? Wasn't he the man after God's own heart? Yet here David stood, face-to-face with an unrealized dream.

As I sat there and reflected on this passage, I realized that David had laid a foundation for his son Solomon to build on and bring David's dream to life. And so perhaps that was the case for me. I realized that day that God was calling me to lay a foundation for others to build upon, and I needed to come to terms with the fact that I wasn't going to experience the dream the way I had always imagined.

I can't describe what I felt as I stared at the pages of my Bible. There was a semblance of peace knowing God had spoken, but at the same time a sense of mourning for a future I thought I had ahead of me but wouldn't come to pass. I didn't know what prayers to pray that could change God's mind. Ultimately, if I truly believed I could trust the Lord with my life, that meant I had to trust him with my dreams too.

Over the next several years, as I learned to trust God more,

God began to show me that our culture has made an idol out of the things we call dreams. And even in the church, we spiritualize our dreams, and put all kinds of flowery language around them, but at the end of the day I had put myself in the center of my dream and used all of the Christian clichés I knew to justify it. I had made an idol of my dream to be a worship leader.

I want to share what God taught me in this season because it's something that I desperately needed in my life. But I believe also that what God has shown me about dreams is crucial for this generation of Christ followers as we seek to honor God with our lives.

Seven years after this moment at the side of my bed, the Lord led me once again to a moment of decision. For fourteen years I had lived my dream of being the worship pastor at Elevation Church. Regardless of what the role looked like, and whether I led worship or not, I loved my job there. But at the end of 2021 I stepped away from my position, and away from that dream, in my attempt to follow God and live out a new dream. For I am learning not only how to let go of a dream but also how to dream new dreams in a way that honors God, and I want to help you do the same with the dreams in your heart.

There is freedom and joy in the words I used to dread: "This dream is not for you." But only after we understand what those words truly mean. They are not meant as a punishment. In fact, these words indicate that God actually has something greater for your life. The key to trusting God in those moments is the realization that your dream is never for you or about you to begin with. You are not meant to be the center of your dream.

And so oftentimes your dream has to die in order for you to see a greater dream come to pass. A dream that was meant for something so much bigger. A dream meant to be part of ushering in the new creation of the kingdom of God in this world.

CHAPTER 2

The Dangers in
Your Dream

Before we move on, there's something you should know about me. A love that is near to my heart is found in a galaxy far, far away. Yes, *Star Wars*. It was a dream of mine as a child to one day assume the mantle as the next Luke Skywalker and learn the ways of the Force. As a man in my forties I have come to terms with the fact that this is a dream that must die, but I am not happy about it. My only hope now is to someday be an extra in a *Star Wars* movie.

One of my greatest accomplishments as a dad is that I have managed somehow to instill in the hearts of all three of my girls a great love for *Star Wars*. They are die-hard, full-of-the-Force fans. And so I was beyond excited to show them one day all of the Star Wars toys that I had collected growing up. Yes, I still had them. All of them. You want a full AT-AT Walker? I've got it. You want a Tauntaun from the planet of Hoth with an opening in the stomach where you can place an action figure just like Han put Luke in to keep him warm? I've got that too.

I couldn't wait to show off these original toys to my three girls. But my excitement quickly turned to fear and trembling when I realized they had different expectations when it came to my "showing them my Star Wars toys." You see, they were under the strange assumption that toys were meant to be played with. As an adult man, I knew the truth—vintage Star Wars toys are meant to be admired from afar. Preferably in a glass case where they are safe from the elements. And so when my daughters went to grab Princess Leia, I intercepted their dirty little hands with a firm "This is not for you! You can look, but don't touch."

Well, if there's one thing my kids excel at, it is persistence. Foiling all their attempts, I continued to stand my ground. "Not only do these toys have enormous sentimental value," I said, "but they also have a potential—although highly unlikely—monetary value one day far in the future." Unfortunately for me, my little girls had a secret weapon, the big gun if you will, and within about five minutes my wife was explaining in her loving yet direct way that toys are meant to be played with, not sit in a box. She also enlightened me that an adult man refusing to share his toys with his children did not put me in the running for father of the year. Needless to say, all of those toys found a new home in our kids' playroom and have been on many exciting yet highly destructive adventures ever since.

LOOK BUT DON'T TOUCH

Many times I feel like God locks my dreams in a glass collector's case where I can only view them from afar but never get the chance to actually touch them.

"This dream is not for you" are words we hear often in life. Whether in the form of rejection, loss, defeat, or failure, being told no is a part of life. And even though I know this fact, I live as if I expect everything that I want to be given to me by God. And when this expectation doesn't line up with reality and I don't get the thing that I want, not only am I disappointed, but I end up placing that disappointment on God and I start to question his intentions toward me. I wonder why he would give me a desire and then lock that thing I want in a glass case. This is one danger of dreams. When we don't get what we want, we start to question why God would seem to tease us and say, *"Look, but don't touch."*

It's hard enough in life to be denied what one wants even if it's something trivial or some small plan that popped into your head on a Tuesday afternoon. But it's truly difficult to be denied your dream. You planned your wedding since you were eight but have never been able to buy the dress. You've dreamed about being a father and watched while every one of your friends had an overdone gender reveal announcement while you wondered inside why God won't let you and your wife get pregnant. You've sent out résumés. You've auditioned. You've written song after song after song, but you feel like you have nothing to show for it. You had a dream that one day your friend would be healed of this sickness and you are now leaving her funeral. When you are being denied your dream, something you've wanted deeply, the pain can be so great that you actually mourn the loss of that dream.

To further complicate matters, it becomes even more difficult when it seems that God is saying, *"This dream is not for you, but it is for someone else."* It's like you are constantly confronted with the dream locked away in the glass collector's case of someone else's life.

This is the story for a number of us, because in many cases we lay eyes on our dreams early in life or at the beginning of our walk with God. Something catches our eye during our formative years, and that dream takes hold in our life and stays there for a long time. And so when we hear "This dream is not for you," we don't feel just mild disappointment. We are devastated.

The story of David helps us to understand these feelings in a better way. If we look again at that passage in 1 Chronicles, we see that David did not just "want" to build a house of worship for God; rather, he says, "I had it in my heart...and I made plans to build it" (1 Chron. 28:2).

His dream wasn't trivial or new. The dream to build a temple wasn't in its early stages of infancy. It had taken root in his heart and was something that had already been acted upon and put in motion. He had made plans. Not vague or general plans, but as you see later in 1 Chronicles 28, he had made detailed plans to build the temple. I imagine this dream was likely birthed in his heart years before when he was dreaming about becoming king. He may have thought building a temple would be his greatest act of significance and purpose, or believed this to be his greatest act of worship for God. His dream was meant to honor the Lord.

At this point it needs to be said that dreams often aren't bad things. In fact, they can be very good things. They can be beautiful. Dreams are one way God might speak to us. They can stir us up to use our gifts and passions for God's glory. God-given dreams have birthed churches, art, music, humanitarian efforts, and justice initiatives. Through dreams God often moves his people to take action. Dreams can drive us to serve God in new, exciting, and fulfilling ways.

But the problem is that the greater the potential the dream has for good in our eyes, the greater the confusion when God seems to say no. David had to be completely caught off guard by the message Nathan relayed back to him. The dream to build the temple was in David's heart *for* God. As David said, it would be "a place of rest for the ark of the covenant of the LORD, for the footstool of our God" (1 Chron. 28:2). But still God said no to David. The dream was not in God's heart for David.

Of course it doesn't always work that way. There are many examples of God placing a dream or burden in someone's heart, and the dream is also in God's heart for that person to carry it out. Look at the book of Nehemiah: "I went to Jerusalem, and after staying there three days I set out during the night with a few others. I had not told anyone what my God had put in my heart to do for Jerusalem" (2:11–12).

Nehemiah had a dream to rebuild the city of Jerusalem, which he did, and his dream started with a burden God had placed in his heart.

And so the issue we are here to wrestle with isn't whether dreams are good or bad. Or whether a specific dream is noble or worthwhile for advancing the kingdom of God. The question all of us are forced to wrestle with at one point in life, usually multiple times, is this: Is the dream in my heart also in God's heart for me?

The question "Is this a no from God, or just a no for now?" is a bit above my pay grade and understanding. As much as I would like to know the answer to that in my life and whether the desires God has placed in my heart will manifest into reality one day, I cannot see the full picture. I don't know the whole story. And that's not the underlying issue we need to address either.

What I do know is that a small lie can come into our minds when trying to discern whether the fulfillment of a dream is God's plan and will, and that lie is *I want it too much*. Is that why God is keeping my dream out of reach? I must confess that I have fallen into this trap before, when I believed that just because I wanted something meant God didn't want it for me. If you get lost in that same headspace, let me say this very clearly: Just because you want your dream to come to life is not an indication that God *doesn't* want it for you. That is bad theology and not the heart of God for his children. He is not cruel. He isn't out to tease us or trick us. He does not do what I did with my girls, showing them my Star Wars toys but not letting them play with the toys. And so we can be confident that he's not parading around desires that he's placed in your heart just to tell you, *"This is not for you."* In fact, he makes known his heart for us:

> Which of you, if your son asks for bread, will give him a stone? Or if he asks for a fish, will give him a snake? If you, then, though you are evil, know how to give good gifts to your children, how much more will your Father in heaven give good gifts to those who ask him! (Matthew 7:9–11)

THE LESSON OF LIMITATIONS

As a dad, I want my three girls to see all their dreams come true. I want them to have the desires of their hearts. And I want them to use every gift and opportunity in front of them for the glory of God. For it is pleasing to God when he sees his children maximizing the life, creativity, and resources he has given them.

But I also have to teach my children limitations. They need to understand that in this life not everything in their hearts will come to pass. Though this is not what we want to hear, it is a fact of life. And this reality has to be held in tension with the popular mantra of "Follow your dreams." Some dreams are realized, while others aren't. It doesn't matter how much I want it, I will never be in the NBA. No matter how many hours I practice free throws, I don't have the athletic gifting for it. Or the height for that matter. I might want it, but it's not in the cards for me. That's not a dream. That's a delusion. And we don't want to live life in a delusion but rather in reality.

While sometimes our dreams aren't realistic because of our own limitations, other times they're not for us because of a limitation God may have set. Maybe the limitation is there because of something he is working out in our character. Maybe we're bumping up against a wall because the dream is meant for someone else to accomplish. Or perhaps we just don't have the capacity to handle what's required of us to accomplish the dream. Perhaps the road to living the dream could lead to heartache or sin. Ultimately, our dreams may be good but not what's best for us.

Though we may not ever know in this life the reason why our dreams aren't a reality, we do know that God is our Father and is good. Just like in my life, no matter how much I want to give my children something good, sometimes the best thing I can do for them is to withhold something they want because it's not best for them. My love for my children is expressed just as much through what I limit as through what I give.

Therefore, we must learn to live in the reality as children of God that both the dreams that have been withheld and the dreams that we obtain are equal expressions of the Father's heart toward us.

LIVING WITH A LIE

I'm obsessive about the things that I love. In fact, I have what you may call an addictive personality. One of my loves is soda. I really enjoy a good caffeinated beverage. Especially a really cold can of Diet Coke. I love it. Like the I-used-to-drink-ten-Diet-Cokes-a-day kind of love it. I can already feel the judgment in some of your eyes coming through these pages, but the good news is that over the last five years I've switched to what I am told is a healthier soda called Zevia. Or at least I tell myself it is healthier. But this obsession with soda led me to a very painful experience.

Several years ago when I was in the middle of a meeting, all of a sudden I felt a stabbing pain in my right side. I thought the pain might pass, but it got worse and worse. I resisted using my phone to google the symptoms; the chances were that I would automatically find the worst possible case, the rarest condition that's only found in Brazil in 2 percent of the population, and then convince myself that I had it. But I started to get worried. I tried to make it through the meeting, but toward the end I just had to leave. Ferris, my amazing wife, was working at the church that day and thankfully took me straight to the emergency room.

Once I navigated the wonderful experience that is the waiting room of the ER, I made it back to the doctor and described the stabbing pain, where it was located, and where it was starting to spread to (I'll leave out those details), and he immediately told me that he thought I had a kidney stone. This was the day of reckoning. I knew it was coming as a consequence of all the soft drinks: 10 a day × 365 days a year × the last 20 years = 73,000 carbonated beverages, resulting in one tiny but extremely painful kidney stone.

The Lord in his mercy helped me pass the stone the next day, but I never knew that something so small—only 3 mm in size—could cause so much pain.

Many of us don't realize that our dreams are almost always whispering to us. In a small and subtle voice—so small, in fact, that we don't hear it—our dreams tell us things about us, about life, and about God. You don't even realize the voice is there, but what it is saying can cause incredible pain.

Your dream loves to lie to you. No matter how pure and good the dream may seem, it will repeat this lie again and again without your even realizing it, and it will repeat the lie until you believe it.

In our culture, not just outside the church but even within it, we have let this lie creep into our worldview and theology, and it is leading us further into worry, discouragement, and depression and away from Jesus and the lives he intends for us. And that lie is this:

Your dream defines you.

It seems simple, almost like an innocent mistake, but it is incredibly dangerous. And none of us are exempt from it. We are bombarded with this message from culture every day, and I personally have given this lie, and variations of it, an unhealthy amount of real estate in my heart.

- The lie that the success of my dream is what gives me true significance and purpose
- The lie that achieving my dream will tell me who I really am
- The lie that the failure of my dream screams to me who I am not

You may be listening to this same lie right now, because it's hard to ignore. It points its finger at us condescendingly and says that we don't measure up because of what we can't do or don't do. Our value and worth end up getting directly tied to our dreams—both their success and their failure.

There is tremendous danger when our dreams define us and give meaning to our lives because of this sobering truth: Whatever you attach your meaning and purpose to is what you end up giving power to in your life. You hand over the keys to your emotional, mental, and spiritual well-being, and that power can cause a lot of pain and do a lot of damage.

It's even trickier and less obvious when we can attach some aspect of spiritual significance to our dreams. This lie works its way in and we don't even realize it because what we are doing is for God, right?

I was devastated when I stopped leading worship, because I let that dream define me. If I wasn't Wade the worship leader, then who was I? My definition of myself wasn't that I was a child of God; rather, it was tied to a task and skill that I utilized for two decades but that had a shelf life. And once my gift was put on the shelf, where did that leave me? In pain. And where does it leave you as you stand there empty-handed in your own life?

This is what I have had to learn the hard way: If a dream defines you, it will ultimately destroy you. Maybe not right away. But little by little it will eventually wear you down. When you lose the dream, it will devastate you, and when you think you've obtained it, it will derail you from true dependence on God.

Tiny, seemingly innocent but wrong beliefs can cause us to build an entire theology around what we do for God instead of what he did for us through the death and resurrection of Christ. This lie that we are only as good as the dream we are pursuing and living is contrary to the message of the gospel.

There's a second and perhaps even greater danger that results from believing the lie that we must define ourselves by our dreams. We end up believing another lie—that God is defined by our dreams. This lie says that if our dreams come true, if we get the job, if we find the perfect husband or wife, if we thrive in our ideal career, if we launch the business and can quit our day job, then that means God is good.

But if none of that happens for us, then, as we said above, we start to question the goodness of God. How can he be good if my life doesn't meet my expectations? Is he still good when he is keeping me from something I deem to be good for me?

Small lies have a big impact.

If we aren't grounded in what the Word of God says about God, our dreams, and more importantly, his purpose and dream for our lives, we will end up spending our energy and our days chasing a dream that leaves us constantly frustrated, discouraged, and empty.

However, there is good news. While our world says our dreams should define us, Jesus taught that letting those dreams die is actually where we find life. Let's go back to those verses in John:

> Jesus replied, "The hour has come for the Son of Man to be glorified. Very truly I tell you, unless a kernel of wheat falls to the ground and dies, it remains only a single seed. But if it dies, it produces many seeds. Anyone who loves their life will lose it, while anyone who hates their life in this world will keep it for eternal life." (12:23–25)

Jesus is talking about his life here. He is about to sacrifice his life to bring about redemption and the establishment of his church, but he is also modeling what it means to be a disciple. The way we are called to live our own lives.

One tiny seed, one singular life, holds so much potential, but that potential is only released through its death.

I'll admit, hating your life seems extreme. Jesus also told us to love our neighbor as ourselves, which means we should actually love ourselves a lot, so I don't think he is telling us to literally hate our lives. But we need to spend time exploring this teaching because what he had to say has never been more relevant to our culture and to the body of Christ. Anyone who loves their life, their plans, their ambition, and their dreams more than they love the kingdom will eventually lose themselves in the pursuit of their life and their dream. But if we are willing to plant our lives, our dreams, and our plans in the soil of the kingdom, submitting them to something greater, God can grow them into what he wants them to be. That requires a release of the seed, though, as well as the death of the dream we were holding. Only in the death of our illusion of control and what we want life to be can we be ready to receive the fullness of what God has for us in his kingdom.

Our dreams hold unlimited potential when God uses them to bring about his kingdom purposes on the earth. But for that to happen, we must hold them the way we are told to hold that seed.

And that is why all dreams must die.

CHAPTER 3

The Striving Self
vs.
the Surrendered Self

If you are wondering at all whether it's only the "bad" dreams that must die, let me say it again:

All dreams must die. Even the good ones.

Both our prideful ambitions and our sanctified dreams. Our misplaced motivations and our noble pursuits. They all must die the same death.

I can say this with confidence because of something Jesus said about discipleship in Mark 8:34–37:

Then he called the crowd to him along with his disciples and said: "Whoever wants to be my disciple must deny themselves and take up their cross and follow me. For whoever wants to save their life will lose it, but whoever loses their life for me and for the gospel will save it. What good is it for someone to gain the whole world, yet forfeit their soul? Or what can anyone give in exchange for their soul?"

I can't imagine what the disciples thought when Jesus said these words. They had to be asking themselves, "Did he really just say that we need to take up an instrument of torture and crucifixion to follow him?" This must have been particularly bewildering, because things at that point had been going pretty well. Sure, there was some controversy, but the crowds were growing, and they were seeing miracles. I guess you could say the disciples were living the dream of the Second Temple period. They were not just witnessing the acts of the Messiah; they were his followers. His closest friends. His inner circle. And now they were being asked to carry a cross.

What the disciples won't realize until later is that this moment was a turning point in Jesus' ministry. This was when Jesus turned to face the religious leaders and powers in Jerusalem. Everything until this point had been his ministry in Galilee. The miracles. The crowds. Now he was heading to Jerusalem, to the cross.

This teaching of Jesus is also problematic for us, in part

because of what we've been taught about sin. I grew up in the church, and I'm about as "churched" as one can get. My grandfather was a pastor, my dad was a music minister, and my mom played the organ in church. I even preached on youth Sunday in fifth grade, and something I heard all the time was, "Deny yourself, take up your cross, and follow Jesus!" If you grew up in church, then you probably heard this too.

But in the church we are also taught a lot about our sin, and the need for a savior and justification before God by grace through faith—which is true, and the heart of the gospel. But as a result of the emphasis we put on sin (and rightly so!), I always read these verses as a fancy way to say "stop sinning." In my mind, I always thought that to deny myself just meant to deny my own sinful desires. And so growing up, when I heard these verses I was never that convicted. I was always in church already. I was there every time the doors were open. I thought, *I know I watch MTV and* The Simpsons *when my parents aren't around, even though I'm not allowed to, and sometimes I think about Kelly Kapowski a little too much, but I repented of that at church camp. Overall, I'm pretty good.* I thought I was above average in denying my sinful desires.

I don't say this to downplay the significance of sin. In fact, the older I get, the more I see the depth of sin in my heart. The jealousy I feel when someone else gets the recognition I thought I deserved. How selfish I can be with my relationships. My greed. The list goes on and on. I've often felt defeated by sin, and maybe you are in that same place.

LIVING IN DENIAL

A couple of years ago I was preparing to preach on Mark 8:34–37 and on sin in particular. I shared my sermon with Pastor Steven, and he showed me something I had never seen before in these verses, something that opened my eyes to just how radical this passage actually is. He told me to read the passage again, carefully and slowly, and also to look for the word *sin*. So I did.

"Did you see the word *sin*?" he asked, then continued, "No—because it's not there." This is significant, because Jesus must not be referring to denying our sinful desires or our sinful selves when he calls us to take up our cross. "Sin" can't be the focus of Jesus' teaching here.

Yes, our sin must be addressed. It's a very serious matter, and Jesus was going to deal with it once and for all. In fact, when Jesus spoke these words, he was about to set in motion the plan to deal with that sin for all eternity. That road led straight to the cross. That is where my sin was dealt with. That is where your sin was defeated. Our sin was pardoned by what Jesus accomplished for us on the cross. As a result, all those who call on the name of Jesus are now on the receiving end of God's grace, and we are called and empowered to live a life free of sin as we become more and more like Christ through his Spirit.

But if denying yourself and taking up your cross isn't about turning away from sin, then what is it all about? And what does this have to do with your dreams?

Jesus dealt with sin on his cross. We have to deal with self on ours.

To understand the ramifications of this, we must first consider or tease out the difference between self and sin. We have confused the two so much in modern Christianity that oftentimes when we think of *self* we automatically associate it with *sin*. But that can't be right, because Jesus was completely good and without sin, yet when he spoke these words, he was about to model what it looked like to deny oneself. This means there must be something about denying yourself that has nothing to do with sin. You can actually deny something good, something precious, like your very life, for the sake of something greater.

For Jesus, dying to self meant being willing to sacrifice what he wanted, his comfort, his desires. It meant enduring opposition to obey the will of his Father. It meant losing followers and friends. It meant radical forgiveness and love. And it ultimately meant giving up his actual life for something greater than an earthly reward—he would gain intimacy with his Father and walk in accordance with his Father's will and ways. He knew there was something greater on the other side of his death. That's where his joy was going to be found—in obedience. The death of the one seed would bring about a harvest of resurrection. Jesus knew true life was found in denying himself.

If this is what Jesus models and the path he calls us to follow, then in order to find our life, as Mark relates in chapter 8, we must do the same. We must take up our cross and die our own death. Not necessarily a physical death (although countless Christians throughout the last two thousand years have been willing to pay that price), but the spiritual death of self.

We can't let a dream die if we aren't first willing to confront the larger issue: Are we willing to give up everything, our entire lives, for Christ, believing that doing so is for something much greater?

STRIVING OR SURRENDERED?

Let's break this down on a practical level. When we talk about *self,* what exactly do we mean? According to the American Psychological Association, self is "the totality of the individual, consisting of all characteristic attributes, conscious and unconscious, mental and physical."[1] In simpler terms, *self* is everything that makes you who you are: your personality, experiences, emotions, talents, passions, and dreams. All of it.

Oftentimes we think the self is bad. We likely confuse the idea of "self" with "selfishness." But in and of itself, the *self* is not bad. Every part of you, which was knit together in your mother's womb by God, is good and loved by your Creator. Remember: Jesus could deny himself, and he was without sin.

But all the components that make you unique were created by God and thus have a particular design. For those components to function in the right way—the best way—they need to work as God designed them. And because God is our Creator, his creation should acknowledge the lordship of God, the Creator. This was his design: That we surrender to his authority. That we surrender our whole selves to Jesus.

---

1   American Psychological Association, s.v. "self," https://dictionary.apa.org/self.

Self is meant to be surrendered.

For our purposes, let's call this ideal state of being our *Surrendered Self*. The Surrendered Self is who we were designed to be, going all the way back to Genesis 1:26–27. There the Surrendered Self lived in submission to the Creator, and thus was in perfect union and relationship with the Father. Adam and Eve lived trusting in God's goodness toward them.

However, it didn't take long before a new character came on the scene to disrupt this communion between the Father and his creation. I think you may actually know this character better than you think you do. And I'm not talking about the serpent. Let me introduce you to the *Striving Self*.

The Striving Self first made its appearance in Genesis 3, when Adam and Eve began to consider what it would look like to make a life apart from God. They thought God was giving them something good in the Tree of Knowledge of Good and Evil, but that he was withholding what was best, its fruit. So their heart took on a new posture toward God: They began to strive to take hold of what was not meant for them. This striving was a result of feeling that God was holding them back and limiting their full potential.

You know the story from here. God's good creation, chief of which is us as his children, was led into sin and ultimately broken. It was at this point that the Surrendered Self gave way to the Striving Self, which affected all of humanity. Every person throughout history—including me and you—has taken on this posture of the heart, and now tries to engineer and manipulate a life apart from God. Does this way of thinking and living sound familiar?

- The Striving Self lives in a constant state of grasping for more, being misled by sin into thinking that God's plans for us aren't truly good and that there is something better always just a little out of reach.
- The Striving Self believes that nothing will happen unless we make it happen.
- The Striving Self thinks that someone else winning means we have lost; therefore, it longs for what others have.
- The Striving Self values self-preservation, comfort, and personal advancement above all other desires.

This is the natural pattern of one's life when the self is not surrendered to its Creator. Sin takes over. It controls us. It allows the Striving Self to have free rein over our lives (see Rom. 6)—until, that is, it is broken by the power of the cross of Christ. Remember, Jesus dealt with sin on *his* cross, and when we accept his gift of grace, the power of sin no longer has any hold on us. We are then empowered by the Holy Spirit to not take up sin on our cross, but to take up self. To crucify the Striving Self and its control of our thoughts and actions.

When Jesus tells his disciples in Mark 8 to take up their cross, he is calling them to a life of surrendering every part of who they are as they follow him, putting to death the Striving Self, so that the Surrendered Self can live.

Here's what the Surrendered Self, empowered by the Holy Spirit, looks like:

- The Surrendered Self can be ambitious for more, but is content with any outcome.
- The Surrendered Self can cheer others on when they get a great opportunity, because the Surrendered Self is secure in its identity as a deeply loved child of God.
- The Surrendered Self can endure a waiting season and can resist manipulating outcomes because of a consistent trust in God's timing and goodness.
- The Surrendered Self can work toward a dream, but is able to trust that if the dream doesn't work out the way they intended, they are still able to make an impact for the kingdom by living out the way of Jesus in their current situation.
- The Surrendered Self can live in the middle of its dream and still recognize that the dream is meant to serve the cause of Christ, not inflate an ego.
- The Surrendered Self pursues *Christlikeness* above any dream.
- The Surrendered Self pursues a life that cultivates the fruit of the Spirit—love, joy, peace, patience, kindness, goodness, faithfulness, gentleness, and

self-control—rather than constantly fighting for or protecting its own interests.

While the Striving Self and the Surrendered Self look very different in almost every way, there is one thing they both have in common: self. Remember, the self is everything that makes you who you are. Your personality, experiences, emotions, talents, passions, and dreams. That means the dreams, talents, personality, and experiences that are present in the Striving Self are still present in the Surrendered Self. Your talents didn't change when you became a follower of Christ—but what you do with those talents and how you use them may drastically change. A trait of your personality, say, being a good listener, didn't change—but whether you use that trait to collect and spread gossip or to be a safe and encouraging friend will drastically change depending on whether you are *striving* or *surrendered*.

While we always receive forgiveness and grace from God, this process of surrender is a day-by-day, hour-by-hour, moment-by-moment act of taking up our cross. Even though Christ dealt with sin on his cross once and for all, we deal with our selves daily. This is what Paul was referring to when he wrote his letter to the church in Ephesus:

You were taught, with regard to your former way of life, to put off your old self, which is being corrupted by its deceitful desires; to be made new in the attitude of your minds; and to put on the new self, created to be like God in true righteousness and holiness. (Ephesians 4:22–24)

This means that every part of who we are must die with the Striving Self daily so we can live as the Surrendered Self. Surrendering is an act of self-sabotage, crucifying old mindsets so that we can see things from a new, higher perspective. We are relinquishing control over the things we once loved. Those things may still be good things, things worth pursuing, but they no longer control us. Surrender is a continuous choice to not strive but to surrender in every area of our lives. And this choice naturally has massive ramifications for our dreams as well. Striving is making our dreams happen at all costs. Surrender is trusting God with our dreams no matter the cost.

And so in order to live as the Surrendered Self, we must be willing to trust God with every part of our hearts, including our dreams. For this is what a disciple is: someone who has committed to living as the Surrendered Self in all things. A disciple knows that dreams, like self, can be used for great things, but only when serving the right purpose. Therefore, all dreams must die in the same way that every part of us dies as a disciple— nothing must control us apart from Christ. But that doesn't mean we can't or shouldn't dream or that dreams are bad. God wants us to be dreamers. He just wants us to be disciples first. Surrender is the defining posture of a disciple of Jesus. If surrender is the posture of a disciple, it must be the posture of a dreamer too.

PRACTICING THE PIVOT

If surrendering our life is a process, something we manage daily and even moment-by-moment, then often we'll find ourselves in cycles of striving once again. Though spiritually in Christ—because of what he did on the cross—we have forgiveness for our sins and freedom from our striving, here on earth we still battle sin and the urge to do things in our own way. Thus we must learn to pivot to the Surrendered Self in the moment when we feel ourselves going back to the patterns of the Striving Self. This is what the Bible calls sanctification, walking in step with the Holy Spirit. It is both a supernatural act of the Spirit and also a practical habit of yielding to the Spirit through disciplines and spiritual practices that help the heart, mind, and body shift from striving to surrender. And so as a discipline, we must *practice the pivot*.

Practicing the pivot is the art of daily, consistently, and quickly pivoting from striving to surrender. This takes discipline, because our natural default is striving, not surrender. It takes repetition, consistency, and action. Cultivating a surrendered heart won't happen by accident. That's why it's called a practice. With the help of the Holy Spirit, we can center our focus on our identity as beloved and redeemed children of God who have been given desires, passions, and gifts that are good and can be used for his glory, while also being willing to lay down what is good if God is leading us in a different direction. And it is this mindset that allows us to desire a dream without being defined by that dream.

Ultimately the practice of surrendering our dreams rather than striving for them is a kind of crucifixion of harmful attitudes and their resulting actions.

- Living as the Surrendered Self *is* a death to being self-absorbed. A death to thinking that all of God's plans and purposes revolve around my preferences and the story I want to write.
- It's a death to self-righteousness—thinking that my opinions and preferences are good and right, and should be canonized.
- It's a death to who I think God should be and instead embracing who he has revealed himself to be in Jesus.

But it's also important to know that as we practice moving from striving to surrender in our daily lives, we aren't ignoring our minds, hearts, and souls, which are created and given to us by God.

- Dying to the Striving Self isn't a death of self-awareness. The Surrendered Self is more self-aware than the Striving Self, because it is willing to recognize blind spots and weaknesses rather than hide them out of insecurity. It also is keenly aware of triggers that induce the self to start striving, or to make things happen apart from God.
- It's not a death of self-love. The Surrendered Self sees

how much they are loved by God, and cannot hate what God created and gave his life for.

- It's not a death of enjoying life and finding fulfillment. You aren't condemning yourself to a life of being miserable because you are losing your dreams. Dreams are good in the eyes of God when they are surrendered. The Surrendered Self doesn't avoid trying to live out of gifting and passion. It just isn't permanently crushed when it meets a limitation it has no control of. Instead, our dreams become offerings of worship that can be enjoyed as they are submitted to a greater purpose.

Learning to pivot is learning to live a life of freedom, a life found only in the joy of the Surrendered Self.

As we continue, at the end of each chapter we are going to learn some specific prompts and exercises for pivoting, or *pivot practices*. They serve as tools that we can use to help fix our hearts on right theology, have the right mindsets, and practice discipline in moments when we feel the pull back toward the Striving Self. They are designed to help keep our hearts in a posture of surrender.

Surrender is not a one-time decision. It's a journey that each of us must go on multiple times in our lives, one that we will never graduate from on this side of eternity. But we can learn to pivot our hearts sooner and more effectively when the struggle arises.

The next step in this process is one of the most difficult, but also the most necessary. We must let go.

PART II

Release Your Grip

CHAPTER 4

Dream with Open Hands

It's in 2 Samuel 7 that we find David going public with his dream to the prophet Nathan. Going public with your dream takes guts, but when you're the king you typically don't face much opposition. To his surprise, though, David ends up hearing a clear *"No"* from the Lord concerning this dream:

> After the king [David] was settled in his palace and the
> Lord had given him rest from all his enemies around
> him, he said to Nathan the prophet, "Here I am, living in
> a house of cedar, while the ark of God remains in a tent."
>
> Nathan replied to the king, "Whatever you have in
> mind, go ahead and do it, for the Lord is with you."

But that night the word of the LORD came to Nathan, saying: "Go and tell my servant David, 'This is what the LORD says: Are you the one to build me a house to dwell in? I have not dwelt in a house from the day I brought the Israelites up out of Egypt to this day. I have been moving from place to place with a tent as my dwelling. Wherever I have moved with all the Israelites, did I ever say to any of their rulers whom I commanded to shepherd my people Israel, "Why have you not built me a house of cedar?"'

"Now then, tell my servant David, 'This is what the LORD Almighty says: I took you from the pasture, from tending the flock, and appointed you ruler over my people Israel. I have been with you wherever you have gone, and I have cut off all your enemies from before you. Now I will make your name great, like the names of the greatest men on earth. And I will provide a place for my people Israel and will plant them so that they can have a home of their own and no longer be disturbed. Wicked people will not oppress them anymore, as they did at the beginning and have done ever since the time I appointed leaders over my people Israel. I will also give you rest from all your enemies.

"'The LORD declares to you that the LORD himself will establish a house for you: When your days are over and you rest with your ancestors, I will raise up your off-spring to succeed you, your own flesh and blood, and I will establish his kingdom. He is the one who will build a house for my Name, and I will establish the throne of his kingdom forever. I will be his father, and he will be my son. When he does wrong, I will punish him with a rod wielded by men, with floggings inflicted by human hands. But my love will never be taken away from him, as I took it away from Saul, whom I removed from before you. Your house and your kingdom will endure forever before me; your throne will be established forever.'"

Nathan reported to David all the words of this entire revelation. (vv. 1–17)

Here God says through the prophet, "Your dream is good, David. It's not a bad thing. In fact, it's something that the Lord is going to bring to pass. But he's going to do it through someone else. It isn't for you to do, David."

In that moment, David could let this *"No"* define who he was and also define who God is. That is, David could allow his disappointment to erase from his memory all that God had done in his life, and his kingship, up to that point, and he could withhold his trust in God for the future. Remember, **if we don't define our dreams, our dreams will define us.**

How did David respond, though? Let's return to the passage:

Then King David went in and sat before the LORD, and he said: "Who am I, Sovereign LORD, and what is my family, that you have brought me this far? And as if this were not enough in your sight, Sovereign LORD, you have also

spoken about the future of the house of your servant—
and this decree, Sovereign Lord, is for a mere human!

"What more can David say to you? For you know
your servant, Sovereign Lord. For the sake of your word
and according to your will, you have done this great thing
and made it known to your servant.

"How great you are, Sovereign Lord! There is no one
like you, and there is no God but you, as we have heard
with our own ears. And who is like your people Israel—
the one nation on earth that God went out to redeem as a
people for himself, and to make a name for himself, and
to perform great and awesome wonders by driving out
nations and their gods from before your people, whom
you redeemed from Egypt? You have established your
people Israel as your very own forever, and you, Lord,
have become their God.

"And now, Lord God, keep forever the promise you
have made concerning your servant and his house. Do
as you promised, so that your name will be great forever.
Then people will say, 'The Lord Almighty is God over
Israel!' And the house of your servant David will be established in your sight.

"Lord Almighty, God of Israel, you have revealed
this to your servant, saying, 'I will build a house for you.'
So your servant has found courage to pray this prayer
to you. Sovereign Lord, you are God! Your covenant is
trustworthy, and you have promised these good things to

your servant. Now be pleased to bless the house of your servant, that it may continue forever in your sight; for you, Sovereign LORD, have spoken, and with your blessing the house of your servant will be blessed forever." (2 Samuel 7:18–29)

Here we see David do something that I believe is the secret to releasing control over a dead dream.

He worshipped.

I know I am a former worship pastor and so I am predisposed to say "worship" in the same way we are taught to answer every question in Sunday school with "Jesus!" but David's response here is a beautiful picture of worship in the face of disappointment. David models for us dreamers how to respond to hearing a no from God. He did not complain or grumble or lose faith. Instead, he pivoted, and there is perhaps no greater pivot than to worship.

As he worships, David recognizes that there is something greater in store for him. His dream will be accomplished by God and God will bless David with "good things" for himself, but more importantly, God's plan is to bless the entire house of Israel. David was to play a part in his dream, just not the part he thought he'd play. In order for him to take hold of these greater things, though, he had to let go of the good thing. The dream wasn't for him. It was for something greater—God's glory and God's purposes. And so David had to put to death his place in his own dream.

WHEN HOLDING ON HURTS

A couple of years ago on a Saturday, my wife, Ferris, had taken our youngest daughter, Sydney, to dance class, and so I was watching our twins, making sure I was being productive at home. You might ask, What did our productive daddy-daughter time include? Playing *Star Wars Battlefront* on Xbox of course. After about fifteen minutes of reminding my daughters that I was still the best with a lightsaber, I told them that I needed to go downstairs to get ready for Saturday church.

As I started to walk downstairs, I had my can of soda in hand as always—you remember my addiction? We happen to have a long staircase of wooden stairs with a very hard wooden floor at the bottom. No carpet to be seen anywhere. I also happened to be looking out a distant window to see what the weather was like and not looking at the steps in front of me. It doesn't take a genius to see where this is headed.

On the third stair from the top, everything seemed to go into slow motion, and a few things became crystal clear to me:

1. While looking out our window, I missed a step and my feet were no longer established on the stairs as they should be.
2. I decided that my utmost priority in that moment was to not spill my Zevia.
3. I instantly regretted the above item as my efforts to not spill my drink failed miserably. Soda went

everywhere, and I fell flat on my back, hitting every single stair on the way down.

4. I made a noise I had never made before and have never made since. It was an inarticulate, low moaning howl that I imagined belonged more to Bigfoot than a man of five feet, six inches.

5. I smashed into the hardwood floor on my back and lay there stunned.

The next thing I see is my twins, Adleigh and Liana, peering over the above railing. They proceed to ask if I'm okay, and when I can't talk or respond something snaps in their nine-year-old brains. I would like to tell you that they ran downstairs to check on their precious father, to make sure he was okay. But no—in this moment, they proved that they are firmly in the "flight" camp regarding the fight-or-flight question, and they ran straight to their rooms screaming.

Here's what I realized as I lay in my soda-soaked puddle on the floor: All I had to do to prevent the whole thing from happening was drop my Zevia and grab onto the rail. Simple. Let go of something that I didn't really need and take hold of something stable. But in an effort to save a drink, I lost my balance, along with my dignity, and spilled the drink anyway.

This is a silly story, but it represents a pattern of thinking in my life, and in many cases the consequences have been more serious than a few bruises and an embarrassing story.

I know there are some good things, some Zevias in our lives, that we are all holding on to and that are actually hurting us in the end because they are keeping us from living the lives God wants for us. We hold on to them and still end up losing them. Today God may be calling you to let go, because before he can trust you with the dream in your heart, you have to be willing to let go of what you are gripping with all of your might.

We can't take hold of anything new God has for us if we aren't willing to let go of the old. That may mean there are old plans or goals that must be released. We have to be willing to part ways with a dream that wasn't meant to be. We also have to be willing to loosen our grip on a dream we are in the middle of fulfilling.

I have a friend named Jared who is an incredible drummer. In fact, he dreamed of one day being a drummer for Elevation Worship. He became an intern at the church, and he thought this was his shot to make that dream happen. However, before the door opened for Jared to be a drummer at the church, he was offered a job as a production director. Leadership in the church saw a gift in Jared he didn't even know was there. In this role, he would be leading the teams that created the atmosphere for worship, and so he wouldn't be able to sit in the drummer's seat, where he had always imagined sitting.

Jared wanted to be obedient to God and follow him wherever he was leading, so he accepted the job as the Uptown Campus production director. Now, ten years later, he is the production director for our broadcast location at church, from which the services are sent out to all our campuses and online around the world. Jared wouldn't have been able to experience this front-row seat of ministry if he had held on to his dream at the time. He had to let go of his dream to take hold of what was before him.

Did Jared have to give up playing drums forever? Not at all. He did play drums for our church. He served on drums at midweek services and in other venues. But he did have to let go for a season. And of course there were days when Jared wondered why he gave up on what he loved, but what's interesting is that over the years he discovered that he could learn to love a new dream. When he thought he was giving up his dream, God gave him so much more. He just had to learn to let go.

LET GO OF YOUR POSITION IN THE DREAM

Several years ago our staff at Elevation Church was taught to ask this question regarding any dream: Am I the center or the servant? As I reflected on this question and on my dreams, whether I want to admit it or not, I found that I often place myself right dead in the center of my dreams. Even the noble dreams. Without even realizing it, I act as if the dream is meant to serve me, rather than serving something greater than myself. My ego is often undeniably central.

As a result, I discovered that I am frustrated when my dreams don't pan out in part because my position, in my own eyes and the eyes of others, is threatened. I see a *"No"* from God as an indication that someone else is his favorite. I start to believe that he loves them just a little bit more than me, and I think that they have been accepted while I have been rejected.

One of my best friends in the world is Chris Brown. We joined the Elevation staff in 2007 together to help build the worship ministry. Chris is my favorite worship leader on the planet. He is a talented songwriter, has the voice countless worship leaders in America wish they had, and is one of those rare people who are even better off the stage than on the platform. Chris and I grew up learning how to lead worship on the South Carolina youth camp circuit. I had the Wade Joye Band, and he had the Chris Brown Band.

When we started building the worship ministry at Elevation together, there wasn't a huge difference in the roles we played in the first seven years. Yes, he ended up singing better songs on the albums, and led the anthems at church, but I was right there next to him leading and singing too. As my transition out of leading worship happened, though, the opposite was happening with Chris. He was trusted with more, not less. He was leading worship on tours in arenas while I made sure the details were good backstage. He was writing songs that our church and the world would sing, while I managed the songwriting camps where it happened.

What made me even more conflicted was that Chris was one of my best friends, and someone the Lord had entrusted to me as his worship pastor. I wanted him to do all the things he was doing. I just wanted to do them with him. And when I saw my path headed in a different direction, in my lowest moments I would hear a voice in my head telling me that God must love

Chris more than me. What else would explain the favor Chris was seeing in his dreams while mine were taking a detour?

What helped me in those moments when I would struggle with my own jealousy was advice another friend once gave me when he was struggling with his own envy and with comparing himself with others. He told me to always "be ruthless about making the right heart choice," and that has proven to be one of the best pieces of advice I've ever received. I knew of God's goodness, faithfulness, and perfect plans, and I knew that I had to continue to do my job well and continue to love Chris.

As I look at the story of David, we see an even better example. I am sure David felt the same way about Solomon as I felt about Chris. Of course David loved Solomon as his son, but the sting of watching someone else live your dream is real and painful no matter who is taking your place. And David was human, not a 2-D cartoon Bible character. He struggled just like us. I even wonder if David thought that Solomon was loved more by God. Or if he had more favor on his life. But here is David's response to learning that Solomon would build the temple:

> Then David gave his son Solomon the plans for the portico of the temple, its buildings, its storerooms, its upper parts, its inner rooms and the place of atonement. He gave him the plans of all that the Spirit had put in his mind for the courts of the temple of the LORD and all the surrounding rooms, for the treasuries of the temple of God and for the

treasuries for the dedicated things. He gave him instructions for the divisions of the priests and Levites, and for all the work of serving in the temple of the LORD, as well as for all the articles to be used in its service. He designated the weight of gold for all the gold articles to be used in various kinds of service, and the weight of silver for all the silver articles to be used in various kinds of service: the weight of gold for the gold lampstands and their lamps, with the weight for each lampstand and its lamps; and the weight of silver for each silver lampstand and its lamps, according to the use of each lampstand; the weight of gold for each table for consecrated bread; the weight of silver for the silver tables; the weight of pure gold for the forks, sprinkling bowls and pitchers; the weight of gold for each gold dish; the weight of silver for each silver dish; and the weight of the refined gold for the altar of incense. He also gave him the plan for the chariot, that is, the cherubim of gold that spread their wings and overshadow the ark of the covenant of the LORD.

"All this," David said, "I have in writing as a result of the LORD's hand on me, and he enabled me to understand all the details of the plan." (1 Chronicles 28:11–19)

David might have thought to himself, *I might not be the one to build the temple, but I can still make the plans.* He didn't sulk, but instead did what he could do to further the purposes of God now, in the time he had. He didn't wait around and do nothing until the dream came to pass. He was active. He set up his son, his successor, well, because Solomon would be the one to live out his dream.

We see, too, that David's dream of building a temple was not meant to serve himself—his ego, his ambition, his attempts to display the power of his kingdom and how close he was to God. We know that he told Nathan about his dream, and he likely told others—and so his reputation was on the line in their eyes. What would everyone think? That he was crazy? His reputation was at stake. His ability to hear from God would be questioned. Maybe he really wasn't a man after God's own heart if the Lord picked someone else.

But David did what he could do in the time he had been given so that his son was able to fulfill the dream. He let go of his preferred position so that God's purpose could come to pass.

We, too, must be willing to let go of how important we look to others. We must be willing to let go of how the dream affects our sense of status. Not only when a dream doesn't come to life, but also when one does yet we play a different role than we thought we would play. If the dream is about me, I'm not going to handle a position devoid of recognition very well. If it's meant to serve the kingdom of God, then that makes the shift much easier to accept.

LET GO OF YOUR SILENCE AROUND THE DREAM

Most dreams incubate in silence. David said the dream was "in his heart." That's where all dreams begin and spend their infancy—in the safety and protection of your silent thoughts as you pray and imagine and plan. At some point, though, every dream in the heart has to emerge into the light.

You can think all day about starting a business, but until you share the idea with an investor or business partner, it's just a daydream. You can dream of writing a book, but until you put pen to paper, or fingers to laptop, it's just a series of random thoughts.

Let's take it one step further. Once you write the book, it's still just a file on your laptop until you share it with someone. No matter how much you dream about asking the girl out, and how much you work out and upgrade your wardrobe, she's just a friend until you ask her on a date. Maybe she still remains just a friend, but you won't know until you take a step. The business proposal that will save your company thousands of dollars is just a "what-if" scenario until you send the email to your supervisor asking for some time to pitch your new idea.

Many of us have declared a dream dead prematurely when we haven't even given birth to it yet.

But why do we keep a dream locked away in our hearts? Perhaps it's because it feels safer to let it die there than to risk the rejection of its dying in public. The problem is that you will never know all it can be until you risk bringing the dream out of the dark and into the light.

We can plan, or dream, all day in our hearts, but we can't expect God's direction until we are willing to take a step. As

Solomon wrote, "In their hearts humans plan their course, but the LORD establishes their steps" (Prov. 16:9). That is when the Lord will establish our steps—when we take a step. It doesn't happen standing still in the silence of our thoughts. It happens when we take action.

David didn't get direction from God on the building of the temple until he took action and shared the dream with Nathan. David, despite having all the power and authority a human could have in the kingdom of Israel, was willing to be openhanded enough with his dream to seek the counsel not just of God, but of someone else whom God could speak through. This may seem like a small detail, but it has massive implications.

Many of us live in the frustration of unfulfilled dreams because we have never been willing to submit and open ourselves to the wisdom that God wants to give through others. There are storehouses of wisdom waiting in our family, trusted friends, mentors, and pastors. Seeking out wisdom is especially important because we all have blind spots. I have a blind spot, and you do too. This is where God can use other people who know us and love us to either add fuel to the fire of our dreams, or lovingly make us aware of something we haven't considered, or caution us because they see a different gift in our lives.

I am thankful that I had people in my life who were honest with me and told me that I didn't have Chris Brown's voice or Pastor Steven's songwriting ability. That didn't mean I couldn't sing or write songs, but it did mean I had a ceiling to my ability

I needed to be aware of so that I could figure out the parts of my gift that I could maximize instead of just maintain. I couldn't see it clearly for myself. I had to hear it from people I trusted to tell me in love and honesty.

Breaking your silence about your dream and seeking wisdom doesn't give over your personal agency to others—ultimately your life is accountable to the Lord. And you also have to be wise in the voices you seek out, which doesn't mean you ask only people who tell you what you want to hear. That can do more harm than good. But it is vital to make sure there are people in your corner who love the Lord and care about you enough to tell you the truth from their perspective like Nathan did with David.

Their counsel may give you the extra dose of faith to take the step, just like when Pastor Steven told me he wanted me to teach and preach more. I didn't see that gift in myself at the time, especially when serving under someone who excels in that gift. His words carried weight in my life, though, and gave me courage. Equally, you need the honest words of people closest to you to help you pause and consider if the dream you are pursuing isn't quite ready to go beyond your inner circle just yet.

Either way, we must be willing to humble ourselves before God and others and admit that we are not all-knowing and may have missed something in all of our dreaming. Their counsel may lead us to discover that the dream should be born, but might need to look a little different than we expected.

LET GO OF YOUR EXPECTATION
FOR THE DREAM

There is no greater joy killer than unmet expectations. And if you are anything like me, there is a constant narrative running through your brain that is scoring your day on the basis of expectation versus reality. Was that conversation more confrontational than I expected? Yes. Did I get the compliment I was anticipating about the project at work? Nope. I know my wife is going to give me the signal tonight after the kids go to bed…Is that the signal?…Well, we will stop right there but you get the point. We all have a long list of expectations, and when they aren't met, not only do we allow them to steal our joy in the moment, but sometimes we can spend hours and days replaying the outcomes over and over and trying to analyze why. Anyone else, or is that just me?

This is especially true of our dreams and hopes for our families, careers, or futures. Some of you most likely have the next ten years planned down to the minute, what needs to happen and when, when you will be married or when you will have kids. You likely have a plan for where you will live and how much money you will make. And if you are reading this book, you probably have some expectation for what God wants to do in you and through you, along with who needs to support you and come on board to make your dream happen. If you are an optimist, you probably expect minimal opposition in bringing your dream to life. Or maybe you have an expectation that achieving your dream is going to be unimaginably hard because everything in your life has been difficult. The expectations are endless and are different for each person, custom-built and tailored to your experience.

A common theme in our expectations for dreams is the time-line, which is to say we want things to happen quickly! However, any cursory reading of the Bible, coupled with a healthy dose of life experience, shows us that speed isn't often the modus operandi of God when it comes to timing.

These are the expectations of our dreams built in our heads and hearts. Dreams built on the bricks of expectations stacked upon expectations.

The problem comes when we realize that our God is a God of the unexpected. Abraham didn't expect to be called from his homeland of Ur and told to go to an unknown land and father a great nation. Moses didn't expect to be used by God after leaving Egypt in disgrace and fear as a murderer. Samuel didn't expect God to pick the shortest and youngest of Jesse's sons who was out tending sheep to be Saul's successor. The people of Israel didn't expect their Messiah to preach a message of peace and forgiveness instead of political conquest, or to demonstrate his love through his very own death. And no one expected that same Messiah to rise again from the grave. God is in the habit of defying our expectations.

But we get so tied to our expectations and building our dreams according to those blueprints that we never stop to see if God might be building something different. It soon becomes apparent that the bricks of our expectations aren't as stable as the firm foundation of his purpose. When we cling to these expectations we will never be ready for the surprises God has for us along the way. We love to quote Ephesians 3:20 and say that God can do more than we ask or imagine. Why, then, do we try to limit God to only what we can imagine? His plans and ways are higher, yet we try to limit what he wants to do in our lives to our imagination of the ideal timetable or the ideal promotion and place to live. We expect God to provide every opportunity, but what if God in his goodness is providing protection from an opportunity? If we are holding on to our expectations, we will never be on the lookout to see how our good God is present and working in the unmet expectations too.

It is imperative that we refuse our tendency to limit God based on our expectations. We find this tendency illustrated clearly in the story of David's dream we have been studying: David dreamed about building a house for God, the temple, and most likely David expected that he could do it because he was the king. David never expected that God would want instead to build a different kind of house, a house in our hearts and through the church, made possible only by the coming of the Messiah, who came through David and his descendants. That definitely fits the category of more than David could ask or imagine!

We could spend the rest of the book dismantling expectations, but here's one that most of us aren't aware of but that is more common than we'd like to admit. It is so common that I want to hit it head-on: Somewhere along the way, we have begun to think that every dream is meant to be observed and celebrated by others.

We expect that every dream is meant for mass public consumption. But if the dream is ultimately for God, isn't it enough if God is the only one who ever sees you doing what you are dreaming about? Here's one that hits close to home: Say you are a songwriter; is it enough for you to write songs as an offering unto the Lord? That's a question I had to answer for myself when I was no longer writing songs that the church was singing. Was my dream taken away or was it actually redirected back to the source it was meant to serve in the first place? There's obviously nothing wrong with writing songs for the church that help people worship God. The problem stemmed from a heart that thought these songs were for other people to sing in order to validate something in me, when the songs were really for God in the first place. As I grew in my thinking, I took on a healthier, but still flawed, view of my gifts from God. I viewed gifts like leading worship and songwriting as offerings meant to encourage others, but in reality my gifts were designed to be offered in worship to God, who would then use them to bless others. As I let go of my false expectations, I was able to continue my dream of writing songs for God even if no one ever sang them.

I currently have a new dream of writing a book. In fact, if you are reading this now, you are seeing the reality of that dream come to pass. In writing this book I have had to come to terms in my heart with the fact that even if no one ever reads it, the dream wasn't a failure. It was enough to reflect on the journey

God has taken me on and write down what I have learned, giving these fifty-some thousand words back to him as an offering. It might seem like a subtle perspective shift, but for me it has been quite significant in keeping my heart free of judging the merit of a dream by earthly metrics of success.

It is also true that some dreams are meant for smaller audiences. Not every book is meant to be a bestseller. This might be what some of your trusted friends are trying to tell you in their loving and gentle way. There's only so much we can do to influence who is impacted by the dream. We can remember who the dream was meant to honor in the first place and bring it to the only one whose validation matters. Can we bring all of our gifts, passions, and dreams as an offering to God first, before seeking out who else looks on approvingly?

You may be thinking, *Does this mean God wants me to live with zero expectations? Does he want me to live a life without hope? That doesn't sound very appealing.*

Not at all. Peter, a man who lived for three years having his expectations unraveled daily by the Son of God made flesh, had this to say:

> All praise to God, the Father of our Lord Jesus Christ. It is by his great mercy that we have been born again, because God raised Jesus Christ from the dead. Now we live with great expectation, and we have a priceless inheritance—an inheritance that is kept in heaven for you, pure and undefiled, beyond the reach of change and decay. And through

your faith, God is protecting you by his power until you receive this salvation, which is ready to be revealed on the last day for all to see. (1 Peter 1:3–5 NLT)

I love that. Live with great expectation. Not guarded expectation. Not safe expectation. No. This isn't a call to live without expectation or without hope. Far from it, for in Christ we are meant to live lives of great expectation. Of unrivaled hope, because faith in its essence is the substance of things hoped for. That expectation and hope are rooted and grounded in something greater than our finite minds and dreams, in a Savior who has been raised from the dead and loves to pour out goodness and mercy onto his children in ways we don't often expect. So release your grip. Let go of your expectations. And expect the unexpected.

PIVOT PRACTICE

Pray and ask God to identify where your efforts to hold on to something good are actually hurting you. Depending on the answer, consider the following:

- **Let go of your position in the dream.** Ask yourself this question and answer it honestly: *Why do I want to play this role in the dream? Does it serve me or can I better serve God and others by taking on a different role* *in it?* How can you be "ruthless about making the right heart choice" in your current circumstances?

- **Let go of your silence around the dream.** Select a few people who love you and whom you trust, and ask for their honest thoughts about what God has placed in your heart. Avoid trying to elicit the response that you want to hear, and instead invite candid feedback with humility. Ask God to illuminate any truth that you need to hear, even if you don't want to hear it. What steps can you then take as a result of the counsel you have been given?

- **Let go of your expectations for the dream.** Try writing down how God may be using you and your dream in a way that you didn't expect. Does this offer any new insight into how the Lord may want to use what he has placed in your heart? What is one step you can take now that is in line with the spirit of the dream even if it is hidden? Is there a way you can serve God through the passion at the heart of the dream that doesn't depend on any human validation?

CHAPTER 5

Upgrade Your Disappointment

Doubt is the constant companion of a dreamer.

Did God really give me this dream? Did I make it up? Does this closed door mean I should stop, or do I break the door down? Will anyone show up for this? What if I take this step and make a huge mistake?

The loudest voices of doubt are reserved for the times when I feel like I've fallen flat on my face. Those moments when I'm staring failure in the eyes and wondering what went wrong.

It would be easy to read the story of David and imagine that he got on board with God's plan right away—no questions asked.

That as a man after God's own heart there was no doubt in David when God said no to his dream. But again the Bible isn't a kid's storybook. It is full of real flesh-and-blood people, people who experience the full gamut of emotions. Just read the Psalms to see all of David's very real, very colorful, and sometimes very violent emotions on display.

I think it is safe to assume that David's heart wasn't immediately overflowing with joy when he learned that his dream was for his son. He wrestled with doubt in his heart. In fact, we can know with confidence that David struggled with getting his heart in line with his faith. He writes,

> Teach me your way, LORD,
>   that I may rely on your faithfulness;
> give me an undivided heart,
>   that I may fear your name. (Psalm 86:11)

I used to read this psalm as if David had an undivided heart, until one day it hit me that he was praying this prayer because his heart was divided. There was already an emotional battle going on inside of him. His heart was anything but undivided.

THE UNDIVIDED HEART

The difficulties of the last few years (I'm looking at you, 2020) have revived a struggle in my heart with anxiety, with which I have been battling on and off ever since my twins were born prematurely and we almost lost them. What's more, navigating a pandemic like COVID with a daughter who has cystic fibrosis—she is at high risk for complications due to the virus—has resulted in a constant battle in my thoughts between belief and unbelief. I feel like the father in Mark 9:24 who says, "I do believe; help me overcome my unbelief!"

Not only does David's prayer for an undivided heart seem unattainable, but I find myself believing the messiness of my heart actually disqualifies me from having faith. Or from living the kind of life Christ promises.

That same year, in 2020, the Lord showed me something about my own heart through a passage about John the Baptist in Matthew 11:

> After Jesus had finished instructing his twelve disciples, he went on from there to teach and preach in the towns of Galilee.
>
> When John, who was in prison, heard about the deeds of the Messiah, he sent his disciples to ask him, "Are you the one who is to come, or should we expect someone else?"
>
> Jesus replied, "Go back and report to John what you hear and see: The blind receive sight, the lame walk, those who have leprosy are cleansed, the deaf hear, the dead are raised, and the good news is proclaimed to the poor. Blessed is anyone who does not stumble on account of me." (vv. 1–6)

John the Baptist was the one who announced the coming of Jesus as Messiah. He was the one who baptized Jesus, the Son of God. The one who said famously, "He [Jesus] must become greater; I must become less" (John 3:30). He was so certain, in fact, that Jesus was the Messiah, not only did he declare it far and wide but he was put in prison because of his message. And in this moment, in prison, he's questioning it all.

"Are you the one who is to come?"

Here we see John the Baptist wrestling with what appears to be doubt. "Did I miss it? Did I spend my life for nothing? Did I back the wrong guy?"

What complicates this reading somewhat, though, is that we also see that John "heard about the deeds" of Jesus. So we know that what John was hearing about Jesus actually supported the fact that Jesus was who he said he was. John heard about the miracles. He heard about the healings. He heard about the teachings. All the things the Messiah was supposed to do, John heard that Jesus was doing. So how much could he really doubt? But if he wasn't doubting that Jesus was the Messiah here, why did he ask the question, "Are you the one who is to come?" I'm sure John had doubts. He was human like David. But perhaps what caused John to ask this question was that Jesus was doing it all without him. The thing John had sacrificed for, given his life for, and been persecuted for was coming to pass and he didn't get to enjoy the blessing.

Was John doubting, or was John just disappointed?

Have you ever felt bypassed by the blessing? Like you missed the miracle? Oh, it happened—but it happened for everyone else. "Lord, I did everything I knew to do, yet none of it worked out the way I thought it would. I had my quiet time every day, I attended church every weekend, and I still lost my job. I still got sick. I am still depressed." How do we deal with this kind of disappointment at the loss of our dreams?

Here is Jesus' response to John's disciples:

As John's disciples were leaving, Jesus began to speak to the crowd about John: "What did you go out into the wilderness to see? A reed swayed by the wind? If not, what did you go out to see? A man dressed in fine clothes? No, those who wear fine clothes are in kings' palaces. Then what did you go out to see? A prophet? Yes, I tell you, and more than a prophet. This is the one about whom it is written:

"'I will send my messenger ahead of you,
who will prepare your way before you.'
"Truly I tell you, among those born of women there has not risen anyone greater than John the Baptist; yet whoever is least in the kingdom of heaven is greater than he." (Matthew 11:7–11)

Jesus didn't rebuke John for his doubt, his disappointment, or his divided heart. Jesus commended John. Jesus actually celebrated John. John was charged by God to announce the coming of the Messiah, and he was committed to that assignment, so much in fact that he endured persecution for his message. What's fascinating, too, is that his charge was even on his mind in that prison cell. There, in chains, he was thinking about his assignment to prepare the way for the Messiah: "Are you the one who is to come?"

On this side of eternity I will never be undivided in my emotions—John the Baptist wasn't either. But I can be undivided in my devotion.

Devotion is a commitment or dedication to an assignment, calling, or purpose. It's unified around that purpose. An act of your will and your mind. An act of your heart. One can have conflicting emotions, doubts, and disappointments but still walk in their purpose. There may be some anxiety and discouragement and fear whose voice is louder than you'd want, but in the midst of that noise you can be undivided in your will. In your determination. In your direction. My wife and I have a strong marriage, but there are times when we might not like each other. There are times when the emotions aren't telling us to love and to cherish. But even in those emotions we aim to be devoted to one another.

In the same way, instead of calling into question my faith based on how I feel, I maintain:

I might be disappointed, but I'm still devoted.
I might be doubting, but I'm still devoted.
I might be in the middle of despair, but I'm still devoted.

One way we can express our devotion, beyond just our words, is by taking action, by doing *something*—even something small— that moves us forward in our calling, charge, or purpose. When we talk about God using for our good what the enemy meant for evil, which as Christians we talk about a lot—yes, that requires us to trust and be patient because we may not see how the Lord works it all together in this life. That doesn't mean, though, there isn't a part for us to play.

MOVE IN THE RIGHT DIRECTION

You might be thinking, *How could John the Baptist move in any direction? He was stuck in prison, looking at the same four walls.* But he acted. He found a way. He certainly didn't make an excuse out of the fact that he was locked up.

What did he do? John heard of the deeds of Jesus. And then he sent his disciples to Jesus. He acted against his doubts and his disappointment, and he took those thoughts to the right person.

Oftentimes in my life I make the mistake of stewing on a thought, brooding. I play out every worst-case scenario, over and over. I put thought bubbles over people's heads. I spend so much energy worrying about something without ever taking action and, more importantly, without ever surrendering the worry to God in prayer.

John knew he needed to hear the voice of Jesus in order to process his feelings, and so he acted against them. He didn't decide to renounce his faith and throw it all away. And so we learn from

John that feelings aren't decision-makers, but they can be great indicators. They can get our attention and raise our awareness to the fact that something isn't right.

We usually assume that our feelings are telling us to pay attention to a threat on the outside. And sometimes they are. But a lot of times, when reflected upon, the threat that our feelings warn us about is in our hearts. We think that every negative emotion is telling us we need to change our circumstances. Many times, though, those emotions are really telling us that we need to change ourselves. The same emotions telling us to quit and to stop walking in all that God has set before us can ultimately be motivators to move us in our hearts into greater dependence on and closeness to God.

Feelings aren't the enemy of faith. They are indicators of the opportunity for faith. Feelings, even the negative ones, can be harnessed and redirected. Feelings can work hand in hand with our faith, pushing us toward the direction of dependence.

God meant for us to depend on him, and thus he wants us to bring all of our emotions to him. That is where our faith actually becomes the strongest. Not just when we bring him our joy, but when we bring him our despair. Not just when we bring him our praise, but when we bring him our frustrations—and praise him anyway.

So don't deny your feelings—your doubts and disappointment over the fact that you aren't where you expected to be in your dream. Don't act like the frustration doesn't exist. **God says,** *"Don't deny it. Bring it."* He wants it all. Your feelings don't need to be driving, but they still need to be in the car. You just have to drive in the right direction to take them to the right place.

That's what it means to have an undivided heart. It's not segmenting what we think God can or can't handle. We have a divided heart when we bring the good stuff to God but hold the rest back. An undivided heart is bringing God our faith *and* our fear.

I believe one of the best actions we can take in response to our emotions is to simply find time daily to admit to God what we are feeling. Don't make it more complicated than it is. On your good days and on your bad days, bring your heart to God and re-center your emotions around him. It can be five minutes at any point of your day—"This is how I'm feeling, Lord, but even in the middle of this disappointment I know you are good. Help me to remember that." Moving in the right direction doesn't have to be a big step. We start by bringing our emotions first and foremost to God, but it doesn't stop there.

ASK THE RIGHT QUESTION

One of the things I have learned in seventeen years of marriage is to never take a question from my wife at face value. The reason is that there is usually a question beneath the question. How many husbands can attest to this? When Ferris asks me if I have any plans on Saturday morning, I have learned that it usually doesn't mean she wants to have a fun morning just hanging out with me. I'm ashamed to admit it, but before I tell her that my morning is wide open, I have learned to ask, "What is it that you want me to do, and does it involve a trip to Lowe's?" I skip to the question beneath the question. The question that's not being asked.

What's interesting in Matthew 11:1–11 isn't the question John is asking, but the question beneath the question: "Jesus, are you in this?"

John wants to be reassured that Jesus is still involved in John's life, specifically, his current situation. He wants to say, "Lord, help me see that you are still working, because if you are, I can handle the storm. I can handle the prison. I just need to know that you are with me."

I love the graciousness of Jesus' response. He doesn't condemn John for his doubt. He doesn't punish him for the question. He doesn't even really tell him anything different than what John was hearing already. But Jesus does put John's circumstances into context by quoting something John would have been very familiar with:

> Jesus replied, "Go back and report to John what you hear and see: The blind receive sight, the lame walk, those who have leprosy are cleansed, the deaf hear, the dead are raised, and the good news is proclaimed to the poor." (Matthew 11:4–5)

John would have known exactly what that meant. Jesus was quoting messianic prophecy from the Hebrew Scriptures (see Isa. 35). He was reassuring John that he was the Messiah, and that the kingdom of God was advancing. He helped John see through the lens of Scripture.

John's question beneath the question is the most important we can ask when our emotions are clouding our vision: "God, how are you working in my circumstances? Help me see them the way you see them."

The lens that Jesus gives John in that moment is the Scriptures, the Word of God. And so the Word of God must be our lens. The reason is that it will divide what is true from what is deceiving us. The Word of God helps us to see our dreams from a higher vantage point. Immersing ourselves in the Word of God is how we can see clearly.

Another way to help us see clearly is to humble ourselves before others. This is an easy detail to miss, but before John could ask Jesus for help, he had to ask his disciples and friends for help. They were the ones who had to deliver John's message of doubt. He was stuck in prison. He had to ask them for help.

Sometimes the hardest but most faith-filled question we can ask is, Can you please help me? With that one question, we are acknowledging our need for God, renouncing our striving and acknowledging that we can't manipulate the outcome. We also humble ourselves before others, because often the deliverance God wants to give is through someone else. John couldn't get his message to Jesus without first opening up about his doubt to the right people and asking them to deliver the message for him. We are meant to live in a community of faith.

There are often times when we can't see through eyes of faith because of our feelings, but trusted and godly friends and community can. We can't live lives of faith in isolation. You may be frustrated in your dream because you have never humbled yourself to the right people, admitting what you don't know, or because you have been afraid to admit that you don't have all the skills required to pull it off. Humbling yourself may be what God wants you to do, and he is waiting on you to lay down your pride and invite other people into your circumstances, into your dream, in order to share your dream with them. Some of you may need to bring your feelings and pain to a licensed and professional counselor. I see one, and it has been an incredibly healthy thing for me. But it all starts with asking for help.

There is so much power in that one word. Often the sound that a divided heart needs to make is just one word—*help*. That's what faith sounds like. You may feel like you have zero faith right now, but if you are calling out and crying out to Jesus, you have all the faith you need. If you are humbling yourself before godly community, you are exercising faith. Keep showing up. Keep seeking Jesus. Keep taking each step.

TRUST THE RIGHT DEFINITION

I was thinking this week about when I first realized I wanted to be in a band. My definition of success then was based on how many people bought my album or knew my songs. I mainly just wanted people to know my name. I mean, I called my band the Wade Joye Band. What I will laugh about now with my wife is that I used to sign my promo shots after youth group concerts with my life verse, John 3:30: "He must become greater; I must become less." Can we just pause for a moment and appreciate the irony of signing a promo shot with that verse? It's a good indicator that I didn't quite understand its true meaning then.

In the moment when John is faced with the fact that his story hasn't played out according to his preference or definition of success—in one of John's lowest moments—Jesus says there is no one more successful in the eyes of the kingdom of God. Never. Not Moses. Not David. Not Abraham. John beat out spiritual giants. He had no material accomplishments to show, but he did have a legacy. Because he had fulfilled his assignment of announcing the kingdom of God. Fulfilling his assignment was success. You see, I think many times I have been disappointed because I had the wrong definition of success. Here is how I think Jesus would define success: *Success isn't about chasing personal fulfillment. It's about being faithful to fulfill your assignment.*

That is what made John great in the eyes of Jesus. That made him successful.

As dreamers, we all need to ask ourselves this question on a regular basis: *Is this dream about my own personal fulfillment, or is it the assignment God has asked me to be faithful to?* If we are honest, sometimes even the dream we are chasing is a way of running from the assignment to which God wants us to remain faithful.

The passage from Matthew gets more interesting because Jesus continues to challenge our definitions. He goes on to say that whoever is least in the kingdom of heaven is greater than even John. When he says this, though, John's messengers have already left. This part wasn't for John. It was for us.

Don't miss this: We are not the ones who define success in our lives. We are not the ones who determine what success is, or, more importantly, we don't decide what success isn't. We don't decide if a dream succeeded or failed from the perspective of God. It is not ours to measure or determine.

We can't measure success according to our preference, but we can model it after the example of Christ.

> He made himself nothing
>> by taking the very nature of a servant,
>> being made in human likeness.
> And being found in appearance as a man,
>> he humbled himself
>> by becoming obedient to death—
>> even death on a cross!
> Therefore God exalted him to the highest place
>> and gave him the name that is above every name.
>> (Philippians 2:7–9)

Before he was exalted, Jesus was obedient. To death. That is our model of success. It looks like obedience. Faithfulness. Surrender. Like living a life of devotion to what God has placed in front of us.

Some of you have been in a dungeon of doubt and disappointment, hearing the reports of the great things happening around you and of all the dreams other people are living. And you feel that somehow you missed it. Your heart feels divided between where you are and where your definition of success says you should be.

But God sent me to tell you through the pages of this book that you are incredibly successful in his eyes because you are devoted. You are devoted to your family. You are devoted to your husband. You are showing up and leading your family and providing for your kids. You're a devoted father. You are modeling integrity at your job. You are devoted to purity in high school. You are showing up consistently to serve in your volunteer position. You are doing the little things that no one sees as acts of worship to fulfill your assignment, and God looks at you and says, *"No matter what you see, I see greatness."*

Your emotions might say one thing, but when you are devoted to the relationships and priorities that matter, when you love faithfully, serve faithfully, and forgive faithfully, you stop looking like yourself and start looking a whole lot more like Jesus. That is what the verse "He must become greater; I must become less" is all about.

An undivided heart, a heart that lives on purpose, doesn't happen without a daily act of surrender. It doesn't happen when we hold our mess back from God. We have to bring it all, and moment by moment ask for the Lord's help and for his strength. The hardest disappointment for me to bring to God isn't when I am disappointed by what others have done, but when I am disappointed in myself. This is where the gospel is such good news because at the cross there is no shame. Only love and forgiveness.

If you feel like your emotional mess or failure is keeping you from your dream today, receive the grace of Jesus. Your feelings of defeat do not disqualify you. They make you good soil to cultivate a heart of dependence. Don't let the disappointment keep you away from trusting God and moving forward. Instead, use those feelings to move you further into a devoted life of drawing near to God and moving toward his purpose. Humble yourself before the Lord and others and devote your heart to seeking the presence and purposes of God, for at the right time, the Lord will lift you up.

It's time for an upgrade. There is power in the testimony of someone who takes what was meant to destroy them—their negative emotions—and instead devotes their heart and life more fully to surrender. That's what made John great, and that can be your testimony too.

PIVOT PRACTICE

In which of these areas does your disappointment need to upgrade to devotion?

- **Move in the right direction.** What feeling have you been trying to deny but instead need to bring to the Lord today? Is it doubt, discouragement, frustration, or loneliness? Identify it by writing it down. Then begin to pray with the statement "I bring my _____ today to you, Jesus." Talk to him about it. And then spend some time listening for what the Lord has to say.

- **Ask the right question.** What need do you have right now with which you are afraid to ask someone for help? Perhaps God wants to invite them into your dream through a need you have. Maybe the encouragement or resource or wisdom you need is available if you would only humble yourself and ask. Take a step and initiate the conversation.

- **Trust the right definition.** Spend some time meditating on how Christ modeled success. What did his faithfulness and obedience look like? What is one tangible way today that you model an aspect of your life—a decision, a conversation, an attitude, or an action—after the example of Jesus?

CHAPTER 6

Face the Facts

Dreams aren't always about what you want to accomplish with your own hands. They often are centered around your most important relationships, especially your family. When these dreams are unmet or put in jeopardy, the pain is the worst and often unbearable.

One of my biggest dreams in life was to be a dad, and this was something I had prayed for and imagined since I was young. The dream became more important to me over time and when I got married, it took center stage in my heart.

I remember the prayers my wife, Ferris, and I would pray when we found out that she was pregnant with our first child.

We had all the first-time-parent hopes and dreams, along with the constant terror of not knowing how in the world we were going to handle being in charge of a tiny human. We were nervous, but more than anything else we were thrilled. Life seemed full of endless possibilities. We hoped and prayed for our child to be healthy. We dreamed of decorating the nursery and of the day we would find out if we were painting it blue or pink. What if it was a boy? I knew I couldn't teach him about sports, but he could be my little Jedi in training—that I could handle. If it was a girl, how would I walk her down the aisle one day without completely losing it? I'm quick to tear up during a movie (don't judge), so that wedding was going to take me out for sure.

We couldn't wait for our baby to arrive and to bring him or her home three days later in perfect health. We also prayed a specific prayer daily that our little one would be full of joy and laughter, and we couldn't wait for that to be the soundtrack of our house. We counted down the days.

We soon learned that our dream was going to go differently than what we had expected.

Our dream doubled.

I will never forget the moment when the doctor told us that there was not one, but two tiny humans in there. I'm not sure how we missed that when we heard only one heartbeat just weeks before, but after double- and triple-checking it was confirmed— we were having twins! Ferris and I freaked out—out of both excitement and the utter terror of not knowing the answer to this question: *How in the world are we going to handle being in charge of TWO tiny humans???!!!*

We weren't just having twins, though. We were having twin girls.

Our dreams got a lot more specific as we imagined raising two little girls. The first order of business was to step up my work-out routine so this five-foot-six-inch frame could be somewhat intimidating to future boyfriends.

The second order of business: Start saving for two weddings!

New specific dreams were coming so fast that we couldn't keep up with all the hope and expectation in our hearts. Thankfully we had some time. It was April 24, 2008, when we learned we were having twin girls, and the due date was September 18 of that year. September seemed like forever away, but we also knew we needed those months to get ready.

That timetable, though, shifted in a dramatic way.

The following is a blog post I wrote on June 21, three months ahead of the due date:

I'M A DAD!

On Wednesday night, June 18 the Lord blessed us with two precious gifts—Liana Hope Joye and Adleigh Grace Joye. Ferris had an emergency C-section and Liana was born at 1 lb., 14 ounces and Adleigh was 2 lbs., 5 ounces. They are both beautiful and courageous little girls.

They were due on September 18, so they are 3 months premature and right at 27 weeks. I will tell the full story soon, but the Lord has already moved mightily on their behalf. In fact, Liana's name means "the Lord has answered my prayers."

Please be in prayer for our girls. Liana is the smallest and the sickest, but they both need your prayers. Our prayer is that they would both end up being healthier than a full-term baby and that they would be able to go home earlier than anyone expects. It is our "sun stand still" prayer. Pray that God would give Ferris and me strength to endure the ups and downs that await us in this season.

This was not the dream.

At twenty-seven weeks my wife was rushed into emergency surgery to deliver our twins three months early. Liana wasn't getting as much blood flow and nutrition from the placenta as Adleigh was, and as a result her heart was starting to fail. Both twins would have died if we hadn't delivered right away. They were the smallest babies I had ever seen. We were able to look at them for less than five seconds before they were taken from us to separate parts of the NICU and placed in isolettes where we couldn't hold them. Nor could the four of us be together in the same room. It was excruciating as parents to barely be able to touch our babies as they fought for their lives.

I was confused about many things in those moments, but

there was one thing I knew for sure. This was not what we had hoped for. We were far from the dream we'd had for our family. This scenario wasn't part of our conversations about what it would be like to hold our children for the first time.

Then, on June 22, four days after the girls were born, we got the call we will never forget.

Here's what I wrote on my blog that day:

PRAY

I want to mobilize everyone who reads this blog to pray for Liana. She was diagnosed today with a grade 4 brain bleed. In fact, this is the worst one the doctor has ever seen. The medical prognosis is that she has a zero percent chance of being what we consider normal. This could manifest itself as not being able to walk, talk, cerebral palsy, etc.

Ferris and I believe the Lord told us that the girls will be completely healthy and that He wants to use this situation to bring glory to Himself by healing Liana and completely reversing this condition. In fact, Liana has another brain scan on Wednesday that we are praying will come back normal. We would like people to pray specifically for this to happen.

We are not praying vague prayers because we want to walk in the same faith that the centurion had in Matthew 8.

What a testimony this would be of the faithfulness and power of our God! We want the name of Jesus to be famous in this hospital and to all who hear about this story.

Adleigh is doing great, but she still needs prayer as well. She is dealing with all of the same issues a preemie faces, but is making progress every day. We are amazed every time we see her by how feisty and strong she is.

We are walking by faith in the truth that both girls will be fine. We are resting in the fact that the Lord has the final word over any medical report. Thanks for your faith and your prayers.

On that day, when the doctor told us she needed to meet with us right away and we sat in that room and she said that Liana had a grade IV brain bleed—and it was the worst she had ever seen—I will never forget how she made sure we understood what that meant. Liana would most likely never walk, never talk, and never get out of diapers. The term the doctor used was "vegetable," and then the words "the rest of her life." And it got worse because we were advised to consider taking Liana off life support.

I don't remember much after that moment other than vowing that we would do everything in our power to fight for our little girl. But my next memory is of Ferris and I lying on her hospital bed and holding each other, crying harder than I'd ever cried before. I think we were that way for an hour, and the whole time the question repeated over and over in my mind was *Why? God,*

I know you are here—I have staked my life on who you are. I am in professional ministry. I don't doubt that you are here—but it sure doesn't feel that way.

After about an hour, I got a call from Pastor Steven. I could barely muster the words to say hello as I walked through the halls of the hospital because my wife's crying was too loud for me to talk to him in our room. He didn't expect me to say much. It's what he said, though, that I will always remember. After telling us how much he loved us and how sorry he was, he gave us this Scripture from Romans:

> Against all hope, Abraham in hope believed and so became the father of many nations, just as it had been said to him, "So shall your offspring be." Without weakening in his faith, he faced the fact that his body was as good as dead—since he was about a hundred years old—and that Sarah's womb was also dead. Yet he did not waver through unbelief regarding the promise of God, but was strengthened in his faith and gave glory to God, being fully persuaded that God had power to do what he had promised. (4:18–21)

Against all hope—that's what it felt like in that hospital. It seemed like all the facts were working against our hope. How do you have hope then? How do you have hope when everything is saying your dream is impossible? That was certainly the case for Abraham. His body was as good as dead but God had promised him a son, and through him a great nation would be born. And it took twenty-five years for that dream to come to pass.

Pastor Steven then told us that there were going to be facts and realities in our lives now that we would have to face—surgeries, treatments, and hard conversations. Face the facts but only speak faith in this season. Deal with what you need to deal with, but speak faith through it all.

We were facing facts in our life that we never would have chosen. There are facts many of you are facing as you read this that I will never be able to understand. Facts that aren't just about a dream job or opportunity you didn't get, but instead about a future with someone who now has gone on to be with the Lord. A divorce has left your family in shambles. You dreamed about growing old together but then he left you. You've dreamed about holding your child but have never been able to get pregnant. How do you face those facts and not waver in your faith? How do you stay undivided in your devotion to God when the facts have just shattered your dream?

FACE THE FACTS BUT FUEL YOUR FAITH

We came out of the conversation with our pastor believing that God was going to heal our daughters. Our prayer was that God would do a miracle only he could get the credit for—that the twins would come home healed. And so we told all the doctors that God was going to heal our girls, and many of them looked at us like we were crazy. At times, of course, I had doubts. I wish I could say that after the phone call with our pastor, an overwhelming peace and confidence came over me and I never had moments of doubt or fear again. I wish I could tell you that I was unwavering, with steady emotions through it all. I wish I could tell you that I was able to get my faith and feelings on the same page. Instead, I felt like John the Baptist in that prison cell, needing reassurance that Jesus was actually with me.

The situation kept getting worse. I remember driving home one night from the hospital after Adleigh had a rough day, which was very difficult because up to that point she had been the healthier of the twins. I was upset about Adleigh, but also exhausted and tired of being strong for everyone, for putting on my strong face for my wife, the doctors, my parents, and the team I led at church. In that moment in the car, the wall came down and I despaired. I wept on the thirty-minute drive home, grieving that the miracle wasn't happening the way I thought it would. Liana's lungs were in bad shape now, Adleigh was having breathing and intestinal issues, and Ferris and I were exhausted from spending every second outside of work at the hospital. Here's my blog entry from that night on July 22:

TOUGH NIGHT

Tonight was one of the hardest nights in a while for me. I walked into the nursery around 5:45 to see about 5 nurses around Adleigh's incubator. Apparently she was having some apnea spells after being off the vent and on the bubble CPAP. They had to bag her twice, which is when they manually use this pump to get her to start breathing. They gave her a new CPAP to see if that would help. We basically just watched her for the rest of the night. They aren't really sure why she is having these issues and definitely don't want to have to put her back on the ventilator, so please pray that Adleigh does well during the night on her CPAP.

I don't want to give the impression on this blog that walking through this process is easy just because we are trusting in God. This is by far the hardest thing I have ever gone through and tonight I literally felt at the end of my strength.

I didn't feel full of faith that night as I drove home, and I honestly didn't feel like praying. All I knew to do in that moment when I didn't have words to speak to God was to turn on worship music. I just wanted to drown out the *Why?* that was playing on repeat in my head. I knew God was there—though I couldn't see the evidence that he cared at the moment. But something happened that night while listening to those songs. My focus began to change.

Why? became less resounding in my heart as the *Who* that was with me started to come into focus. That's when I began to realize that if I let my feelings dictate my decisions in this situation, I wouldn't make it through it.

Romans 4:20 says of Abraham, "Yet he did not waver through

unbelief regarding the promise of God, but was strengthened in his faith."

If you study Abraham's life, it seems like he wavered a lot! As I mentioned above, there were twenty-five years between the promise that he would have a son in his old age and the birth of Isaac. I have to believe he was pretty wavering in his emotions during those years of waiting, but he somehow remained unwavering in his belief as he strengthened his faith. Like we said in our last chapter, his heart was divided, but he was undivided in his devotion.

I learned in that moment that I couldn't fake my feelings, but I could choose to fuel my faith. So to strengthen our faith as a family, we put Scripture all over the girls' rooms and on their isolettes—not just as a declaration of what we were believing but as something for Ferris and I to focus on in our freak-out moments.

I had to choose to believe the Word of God over my feelings. Instead of looking for any fluctuation on the heart and oxygen monitors—which the nurses tell you not to look at, but once they tell you, all you can think about is the monitors—I needed to look at the Word of God. I needed to fuel my faith rather than look at a monitor and feed my worry. Though I still to this day have a mini panic attack when I hear a sound that's similar to the sound of those monitors going off, I gradually learned to get better at pivoting from worry to faith.

When I would wake up in the middle of the night full of fear, I'd get my guitar and try to sing something that would give my heart more faith. I'd be lying if I said it wasn't a fight. But if I didn't fight it, my feelings would take over. I had to face the facts. I couldn't deny what I was feeling, but I knew I couldn't stay in that place either. Faith is a fight, but God has given us weapons in that fight to overcome our feelings. His Word is a weapon. Worship is a weapon. The church community is a weapon.

On the night the girls were delivered I was left alone in a hospital room terrified, and a nurse came in and said, "You don't know me, but I go to your church and you have a lot of people praying for you." I never saw her again, but in the moment when I felt most alone I realized my feelings were not the reality. There was something greater than my feelings surrounding me and upholding me.

My church family walked this with me. They fought with me when my faith was weak. The sermons that were preached each weekend sustained me. Worship lifted my perspective. I learned how vital the house of God was because I couldn't have kept my faith without my church. Sometimes you need to borrow someone else's faith when you don't feel it yourself. You need others to fight with you when you don't have the strength yourself. When we don't feel God's presence, we must realize that his presence is in the people he has sent to walk with us in the trial we are facing.

FACE THE FACTS BUT DON'T FORGET GOD'S FAITHFULNESS

Three months after the twins were born, and after four major surgeries between the two of them, Adleigh and Liana came home from the hospital within a day of each other as healthy little girls. I was excited but cautious. I didn't know if a setback would land us right back in the NICU, and so it was tough to celebrate wholeheartedly.

The girls still had a tough road ahead of them, but their being healthy enough to leave the hospital was an answer to prayer. A few months later Liana would get a shunt due to her brain bleed, and she'd deal with mild cerebral palsy, with weakness on her right side, but most people would never notice and for all intents and purposes she is doing everything the doctors said she would never do. Liana came home a miracle. Adleigh would have one major heart surgery, but after that she had virtually no more complications. She came home a miracle as well. I had prayed that their healing would be instantaneous in the hospital—that one day a scan would show no evidence of a brain bleed. A gradual healing doesn't make it any less of a miracle. Gradual healing is still healing.

Ferris and I were incredibly grateful for what God did and for the goodness and mercy he so richly poured out into our lives. Not everyone in the NICU has the same outcome we did. We made friends with people in the NICU whose children didn't make it home. We cried with them. We hurt with them. So we wanted to be faithful to tell people what God had done in Adleigh and Liana's story. We knew it wasn't normal. So we told our story to everyone willing to hear. I wrote songs about it all.

Even after a victory, fights leave scars. I dealt with panic attacks for the first time ever. I was driving one day and had to pull over and tell Ferris I needed her to drive because I thought

I was going to pass out. While leading worship that next Easter, I battled to make it through the worship time without running off the stage. I preached at church one weekend and barely knew what I was saying because I was gripping the podium and praying I wouldn't drop to the floor in front of a thousand people. The effects of the trauma were real.

We were also afraid to have more children. We wanted another child, but we never wanted to see the NICU again. It terrified us. We kept praying, though, and little by little we started to dream again. After four years of emotional healing and prayer, we finally felt the time was right to hope again for another child. We had learned to hope again. We were ecstatic when we found out we were having another baby girl and we decided to name her Sydney.

I can't express how thrilled we were to have the full pregnancy experience we missed out on the first time. We would be able to hold our daughter when she was born rather than have her taken away to the NICU. This time the dream seemed to be going according to plan. In fact, Sydney wasn't early— she was actually about a week late. And things were so good in labor that when I was tickling Ferris's back in the hospital room to soothe her nerves with my right hand, she busted me playing *Fruit Ninja* with my left hand on my phone. Husbands, I don't advise that you play video games while your wife is in labor. I admit this was not my best moment of support. But it shows how relaxed we were—well, at least I was. Or, at a minimum, how different this delivery was compared to the delivery of Adleigh and Liana. (I don't want any woman who has experienced labor to hunt me down.)

Sydney was born and was beautiful. She looked like a giant at birth compared to the twins when they were born. She wasn't immediately taken from us either—we got to hold her. It was perfect.

I remember that it was election night in 2012, and I was holding Sydney watching the news while Ferris slept. I was overcome with gratitude. We had dared to dream again and I was holding that dream in my arms.

As I sat there, thankful, I noticed that Sydney started to have a coughing fit. That in and of itself wouldn't be too alarming, but I looked down at her and saw that she was coughing up blood. I hit the button to call the nurse faster than I've ever done anything in my life, and chaos ensued. Doctors rushed Sydney out of the room to run tests. I was disoriented, but not more than Ferris, who had woken up to her baby being taken away. One minute Sydney was with us, happy and healthy, and the next she was nowhere to be seen. She had gone to the place we never wanted to see again, the NICU. Sydney's intestines had ruptured and she needed emergency surgery. I felt like I was living in a nightmare. Everything in me was crying out, *How can this be happening again?!*

I tried to tell myself that this was just a scare, that surgery would fix the problem, and that soon we'd get to go home. But one night turned into a week, which turned into two weeks, and then five. Throughout that time, our amazing medical team in the NICU worked tirelessly to figure out what was wrong with Sydney. There were many possibilities, and the longer she was there, the scarier things got. One possibility that was mentioned, which was a worst-case scenario, was cystic fibrosis. We didn't know much about the disease, but what the doctors were saying about it terrified us. We knew we didn't want that to be the diagnosis. I tried to be confident that surely she didn't have cystic fibrosis, especially because we had already been through our trial with the twins.

One afternoon after work as I was driving to the hospital, I got a call from Ferris, who was in tears. It took me what seemed like forever to make out what she was saying, but eventually five syllables came through loud and clear—cystic fibrosis. I was devastated. I knew what the doctors said about the disease and I had done my own research on it, and so I knew the prognosis wouldn't be good. If you don't know what CF is—it's typically referred to as just CF—you're not alone. Most people aren't familiar with it, mainly because it's rare. Only about thirty thousand people have it in the United States at the time I write this. CF is a terminal genetic condition that currently has no cure. It affects your lungs and digestive system the most. Decades ago most kids with CF didn't make it to elementary school age, but thankfully today the average life expectancy is close to forty. Progress is being made every year, but we were told that most people with CF end up with extreme lung issues and often have to get lung transplants. Even though treatments have improved, what would be a normal cold to us can send a child with CF to the hospital in serious condition.

We were shocked and terrified. Here we were again, back in the NICU, back in the place we never wanted to be again. What do you do when you win the fight once but you find yourself back fighting against similar facts, which seem even more insurmountable than the ones you faced the last time?

In that moment I have never felt more abandoned by God. Ferris and I didn't blog at the time. There are no journal entries to share. If there were, they would be full of anger, sadness, frustration, and disappointment. I felt let down and betrayed by God. My feelings, which I know can't be trusted, said, *God, how could you let us go through all that with the twins, get the courage to have another child, and then now we are facing the fact of raising a little girl who may not make it to her twentieth birthday. Why?*

It took four years to rebuild our courage to have another child, but it took only a four-minute conversation to turn our triumph into a tragedy. We had gotten the courage to dream again, and now we were confronted again with all the doubt and disappointment from our time in the hospital with the twins. And the sting of this disappointment felt worse.

I know many of you are facing facts that are far more difficult than any I have faced, and you could teach us far more about faith than I ever could. And some of you feel now that you are in a difficult place again. You can't believe God would allow you to be here again.

Maybe you feel the way David felt when he wrote the following prayer:

> Will the Lord reject forever?
>   Will he never show his favor again?
> Has his unfailing love vanished forever?
>   Has his promise failed for all time?
> Has God forgotten to be merciful?
>   Has he in anger withheld his compassion?
>   (Psalm 77:7–9)

Aren't you grateful that the Word of God shows that it's okay to feel this way sometimes? David, the man after God's own heart who seemed to navigate so maturely after being told no to his dream of building the temple, felt at times abandoned by the Lord. He hit rock bottom too. What he says in the next verse is what pulled me out of my darkness:

> Then I thought, "To this I will appeal:
> the years when the Most High stretched out his right hand.
> I will remember the deeds of the LORD;
> yes, I will remember your miracles of long ago." (vv. 10–11)

I will remember.

Those three words shed a little light into my darkness. I realized my question was all wrong. Instead of saying, "God, why am I going through this when I've been through this before?" I needed to flip the question into a statement: "God's going to get me through this because I've been here before."

After being told by Nathan that he couldn't build the temple, David puts this psalm into practice by remembering God's faithfulness to Israel in prayer:

And who is like your people Israel—the one nation on earth that God went out to redeem as a people for himself, and to make a name for himself, and to perform great and awesome wonders by driving out nations and their gods from before your people, whom you redeemed from Egypt? (2 Samuel 7:23)

He also declares God's faithfulness to his own family line as he later commissions Solomon to build the temple:

Yet the LORD, the God of Israel, chose me from my whole family to be king over Israel forever. He chose Judah as leader, and from the tribe of Judah he chose my family, and from my father's sons he was pleased to make me king over all Israel. (1 Chronicles 28:4)

In each instance, David put his focus on God's past faithfulness.

So that's what Ferris and I tried to do. We sought to remember God's faithfulness with the twins, and to trust that the same God who was with us then was with us now. Of course, we wouldn't have chosen these facts. There are times in everyone's life when the facts being faced wouldn't have been chosen. In life, we often can't choose our facts. What we can do, though, is choose what we focus on and what we remember.

When Sydney was eighteen months old, she was having trouble gaining weight. This is common for kids with CF, and so she received a gastrostomy tube, through which she would be given special formula at night while she slept. A gastrostomy tube, commonly called a G-tube, looks like something you would use to blow up a pool float, and it's attached to a small hole in the stomach. Sydney affectionately calls her G-tube her "tubey."

Part of the G-tube has to be changed every three months, but sometimes it just pops out. When this happens the small hole in Sydney's stomach is open. (This sounds way worse than it is.) And we are supposed to get a new tubey in there before the hole starts to close on its own. Apparently the body doesn't like an open hole that goes directly into the stomach. Who knew?

One day Sydney was with my parents when the tubey came out. Unfortunately, they had no spare tubeys with them and they weren't near our house, so they went to the hospital. The hospital they went to, though, didn't have the right one, which resulted in my having to leave work and break numerous speed laws to get to my house, pick up a spare tubey, and then race across town to this hospital, hoping to deliver the tubey before the hole started to close. Once it closes, that means another surgery.

Thankfully, I got it there just in time. But by the time I walked into Sydney's hospital room, she was officially in full-fledged freak-out mode. She never liked getting her tubey replaced under normal circumstances—it was painful—but now, because of all the drama, she was very upset and terrified. It broke my heart to see her this way. As we tried to insert the new tubey, the more she moved, and the more difficult it became for the doctors and the more painful it ended up being for Sydney. They couldn't get the tubey in while she was fighting them and me. I will never forget the way she looked up at me, screaming, "Daddy, please make it stop! Daddy, please, it hurts!"

The whole time I was as close as I could be to her, telling her that it would be over soon if she just trusted me and stopped fighting. It felt like an eternity. She kept fighting, and kept screaming, until she finally just surrendered. She stopped fighting, stared up at my face, looked me in the eyes, and the tubey went right in. She was fine.

Though the crisis was averted, I was driving home that night and once again asked God, *Why?* This seemed to be becoming a pattern in my night drives home from the hospital. I was asking God legitimate questions: *Why does Sydney have to have cystic fibrosis? Why is this her reality?*

The Lord spoke to me clearly in the car that night—Sydney's response to me and the doctors that day was like my response to God. I had been spending all my energy fighting the wrong thing. Instead of fighting my feelings, or fighting for my faith, I was fighting God by trying to avoid what he wanted to walk through *with* me. However, the more I fought, the longer it hurt. Instead, he simply wanted me to trust him. I had never understood trust the way I did at that moment. I was right there with Sydney, in her pain and in her fear, and I was going to get her through it if she would just stop fighting and surrender.

Sydney finally became calm when she zoned in on my face. Looking into my eyes caused her to pivot toward trust and surrender. As long as I could keep her looking into my eyes, at my face, in the midst of the facts, she was able to trust. In the same way, I can face any fact as long as I keep my eyes on God's face.

FACE THE FACTS BUT FOCUS ON HIS FACE

I don't know what the future holds for my girls, but I can tell you that Sydney and the twins are healthier than I ever could have imagined. They are walking daily reminders of God's miracle-working power. In my darkest moments, in my despair, I wasn't able to take into account this power, which is also a fact, more real than the facts I was facing.

The ultimate fact of the matter was that God was with me even when the facts were stacked against me. And through it all, God was inviting me into his presence in a deeper way than I had ever experienced.

What Paul wrote to the church in Corinth made more sense to me then:

> We are hard pressed on every side, but not crushed; perplexed, but not in despair; persecuted, but not abandoned; struck down, but not destroyed. (2 Corinthians 4:8–9)

Some of you are facing hard facts in your lives, and these facts are real—real pain, real loss, real heartache. Each day you wake up and they are there. There's no escape. Each day you have to face them. You have to get out of bed, you have to go to work, and you have to care for your loved ones. And there are days when you feel like you can't face the facts. The word of the Lord for you today is that he is with you. He will never leave or forsake you. Keep your focus fixed firmly on him when nothing around you seems to make sense, because your facts don't tell the whole story.

No matter the details of your trial, God is there, he loves you, and he promises to work all things for your good. He sees your situation, and he will act on your behalf. **He sees the facts that you face, but he sees them from a different vantage point.** That's where true hope is found. **So we face the facts but we don't take the facts at face value.** We don't judge the journey before it's over. And we never judge the story God is writing in our lives by the scenes we are in. We know he is there. We know he is at work.

God wants you to see his face in the middle of your facts. As the old hymn says,

> *Turn your eyes upon Jesus,*
> *Look full in his wonderful face,*
> *And the things of earth will grow strangely dim*
> *In the light of his glory and grace.*[1]

---

1   "Turn Your Eyes upon Jesus," words and music by Helen Howarth Lemmel, 1922.

I don't know what the future holds for you, but I do know that Jesus has been faithful, is faithful, and will always be faithful. These are the facts that you can stand on no matter how you feel.

PIVOT PRACTICE

- **"Against all hope, Abraham in hope believed."** What facts are you currently facing that are robbing you of hope?
- **Fuel your faith.** Identify the places and times when you are most likely to be triggered by your facts and lose hope. We put index cards with Scriptures all over the hospital rooms of our girls to pivot to trust when our hope was slipping away. Write down a few Scriptures to cling to on your own index cards and place them where you will see them and say them out loud daily as part of your routine or in a moment of doubt or weakness. If you don't know where to start, write down Romans 4:18–21.
- **Remember God's faithfulness.** One of the greatest ways to fuel your faith is to remember what God has done. I can't tell you how many times I have gone back and reread the blog posts we wrote during

our twins' time in the hospital to remember how God has been with us and answered our prayers. You don't need a blog to do that. Spend time writing down pivotal moments in your life where God moved on your behalf or answered a prayer, or where you can see in hindsight clear evidence of his goodness and faithfulness. Once you have a list started, make it part of a regular prayer time to say it out loud and thank God for his past faithfulness in your life. Commit it to memory. When a new challenge or trial comes, say, "The God who did _____ and was with me then is with me now and will deliver me."

PART III

Reclaim
Your Purpose

CHAPTER 7

Notice Your Narrative

There is a narrative about your life that you have accepted. It's a narrative that interprets your past and hyper-focuses on your future. This narrative usually has a lot to say about your significance and perceived importance in the world around you. And it exists solely in your mind. The narrative you choose to believe is powerful, because daily it either pushes you toward a life of striving or pivots you back toward surrender.

Take a moment to notice your narrative. Do you think of yourself as the underdog or the hero in your story? Are you the victim or the person who tends to get whatever they want? What is the purpose of your plotline? What is the great journey your character is on? Where is that path headed, and where do you believe it's destined to end?

It's important to be aware of our narrative, because much of our frustration in life comes from the fact that our day-to-day lives don't match the narrative we have written in our heads. We think we are meant for certain grand accomplishments, or certain comforts and freedoms. We believe there is a purpose for us out there just waiting to be discovered. But when our path takes us further from, instead of closer to, this purpose we are working so hard to find, we are led to a life of endless striving. We will do anything to get back on track, anything to return to the path that leads what we believe is our purpose.

Returning to David, notice how the Lord reframes David's perspective. He redefines David's life and story in the context of a greater narrative. A narrative much bigger than the one David had written for himself.

First, he reminds David whose hand has brought him this far:

> Now then, tell my servant David, "This is what the LORD Almighty says: I took you from the pasture, from tending the flock, and appointed you ruler over my people Israel. I have been with you wherever you have gone, and I have cut off all your enemies from before you. Now I will make your name great, like the names of the greatest men on earth." (2 Samuel 7:8–9)

Then, after recalling to David's mind how good he has been to him up to this point, God begins to broaden his perspective beyond David himself:

And I will provide a place for my people Israel and will plant them so that they can have a home of their own and no longer be disturbed. Wicked people will not oppress them anymore, as they did at the beginning and have done ever since the time I appointed leaders over my people Israel. I will also give you rest from all your enemies.

The LORD declares to you that the LORD himself will establish a house for you: When your days are over and you rest with your ancestors, I will raise up your offspring to succeed you, your own flesh and blood, and I will establish his kingdom. He is the one who will build a house for my Name, and I will establish the throne of his kingdom forever. I will be his father, and he will be my son. When he does wrong, I will punish him with a rod wielded by men, with floggings inflicted by human hands. But my love will never be taken away from him, as I took it away from Saul, whom I removed from before you. Your house and your kingdom will endure forever before me; your throne will be established forever. (2 Samuel 7:10–16)

God emphasizes a crucial detail, making sure David understands that this dream is not limited to just David. That's much too narrow of a scope. To paraphrase, the Lord tells David, *"This dream is my dream and it's meant to bless the people of Israel. And from Israel it will bless the world. What I am doing through you is giving Israel a safe home. And in this home, there is something even greater I want to build."*

David wanted to build a house for God, but God wanted to build a house through David. In the Scriptures a "house" could refer to a place of worship, but it could also refer to a family, and God was building both. Solomon would be David's successor who would not only build the temple but also firmly establish the royal line from which the kings of Judah would descend. And while most of those kings would not be considered a blessing, there would be a king who would descend from David's line, Jesus, who would bless all the people of the world and establish through his own death and subsequent resurrection an everlasting house—a new family of God—the church.

David saw in his mind only his story, and he wanted it written in a certain way. But God saw a greater story, one that he was writing through David. David imagined what his hands could build *for* God. But God wanted David to see that the death of his dream would ultimately be for God and for others. David's part in God's plan was for something much bigger than David realized. Though it wasn't David's narrative, God wanted to write a much larger narrative through David's life if he would stop striving and surrender.

The process of defining our dreams first starts with defining their place in the larger story that God is telling. Only then can we see our dreams and ourselves properly. We have to realign our hearts with the heart of God. We may have dreams in our hearts, but he has a purpose in his. It's our responsibility to search our hearts and motives to ensure that our dreams align with his purpose. That's exactly what David did when he responded in prayer:

> For the sake of your word and according to your will, you have done this great thing and made it known to your servant.
>
> How great you are, Sovereign LORD! There is no one like you, and there is no God but you, as we have heard with our own ears. And who is like your people Israel— the one nation on earth that God went out to redeem as a people for himself, and to make a name for himself, and to perform great and awesome wonders by driving out nations and their gods from before your people, whom you redeemed from Egypt? You have established your people Israel as your very own forever, and you, LORD, have become their God. (2 Samuel 7:21–24)

David acknowledges a greater purpose than building the temple. By framing his life within God's larger narrative, he takes the first step in addressing the ultimate question behind every struggle with our dreams: *What exactly is God's purpose for my life?*

This question is crucial, because the culture has given us a narrative that says life is about chasing our own personal fulfillment. That is the wrong narrative, and it's time we got back to the right one. The kingdom of God isn't about personal fulfill-ment. It's about God fulfilling his purposes in us and through us.

THE POWER OF BEING PORTABLE

If you were in high school in the early '90s like me, then chances are good you spent regular time at Bayside High while watch-ing *Saved by the Bell*. Besides being envious of Zack Morris's hair and his relationship with Kelly Kapowski, I also wanted his high-tech, state-of-the-art mobile phone. I can't use the term "cell phone" because that suggests the image of a phone that fits easily into your pocket, which was not the case with Zack's piece of advanced technology. I am talking about a phone the size of my toaster. It was massive.

Well, back in 1993, I lived my dream. I was one of the first kids at Spring Valley High School to get one of those mobile phones, except mine was slightly different. Mine was attached to my car. It was a car phone. I thought I was the envy of all my friends—my go-to pickup line was to ask girls if they wanted to take a ride in my red Toyota Celica to check out my car phone. The line wasn't always very successful, but you can't fault me for trying.

I soon came to the realization, though, that I was tricked by my parents because now I had no excuse to not check in with them no matter where I was. It wasn't just a car phone. It was a parental leash. But I didn't care because to my high school mind, the pros definitely still outweighed the cons.

In those days I worked at a Christian camp in Ridgeway,

South Carolina, called Camp Longridge, and my mission every night after the campers went to bed was to call my girlfriend from my car phone—because who would want to use the regular landline in the canteen? I could bypass the line of people waiting to use the phone because of my coveted car phone. But there was one problem. For those of you born after the turn of the century, you may not realize that a cell phone signal was far from a sure thing in the early '90s, and out at the camp I couldn't find a signal. I tried everywhere on the grounds but had no luck. I drove around the cabins, down to the lake, and out by the chapel. Nothing. No signal. Until one night I drove my car to the one place I hadn't tried—the middle of the softball field. I proceeded to drive over every square inch of that field until I found the one small spot that somehow, miraculously, had a signal. If you were not parked in this exact spot, you were out of luck, but if you were in the sweet spot, you could talk all night. For the rest of the summer that became my new nightly routine—until my parents got the car phone bill. My late-night softball-field calls then came to an abrupt end.

But due to the Lord's great mercy the days of my car phone are long gone, and we are living in the glory of the iPhone. (Or Android if you haven't gotten saved yet.) My iPhone is a massive upgrade from my car phone in almost every way, but perhaps the greatest improvement is that it is 100 percent portable. It isn't bound by the limitations of where I can drive my car. I can't take my car into church with me. I can't take it on an airplane. But not only can I take my current phone anywhere, it actually works pretty much everywhere. I have taken my iPhone all around the world, and whether I am in Charlotte or in Israel, I can get a signal and I can have a conversation. I can send a text. It is truly portable because it works everywhere.

Whether or not we should have a cell phone that makes us accessible at all times is another question, but I do think this little story illustrates a truth that's key to our discussion at hand. You see, I used to think that my purpose—the call of God on my life—was like my old car phone. It was something that worked only under ideal conditions. That is, life had to look a certain way for God to truly achieve through me what he wanted. I believed that I could make a difference only if I had the perfect job, the perfect family, and the perfect testimony, if I was in the place and position of my preference. When all those conditions were right, then I could live out my purpose. To say it another way, my dream was my ultimate destination, and if I achieved my dream, only then could God use me. Or in the reverse, I thought an unrealized dream would lead to a derailed destiny, which created an extreme amount of pressure on living in my preferences.

Thankfully, the Bible teaches that the purpose of God for our lives is more like my iPhone than my car phone. It is meant to work everywhere.

The purpose of God for you wasn't derailed if you didn't end up where you thought you should be. The purpose of God for your life isn't contingent on your plans or the opportunities that other people give you or don't give you. Your purpose is portable—you carry it with you in the season of victory and you carry it with you in the seasons of discouragement and trial. You can live in your purpose even if you aren't living in your dream.

But to do this we must understand the narrative God is writing, and we must see that narrative from the beginning: "In the beginning God created the heavens and the earth." Here's what the very first chapter of Genesis says about God's purpose for us:

> Then God said, "Let us make mankind in our image, in our likeness, so that they may rule over the fish in the sea and the birds in the sky, over the livestock and all the wild animals, and over all the creatures that move along the ground."
>
> So God created mankind in his own image,
>> in the image of God he created them;
>> male and female he created them.
>
> God blessed them and said to them, "Be fruitful and increase in number; fill the earth and subdue it. Rule over the fish in the sea and the birds in the sky and over every living creature that moves on the ground."
>
> Then God said, "I give you every seed-bearing plant on the face of the whole earth and every tree that has fruit with seed in it. They will be yours for food. And to all the beasts of the earth and all the birds in the sky and all the creatures that move along the ground—everything that has the breath of life in it—I give every green plant for food." And it was so. (Genesis 1:26–30)

The biblical narrative begins with a beautiful picture of God creating man in his image and tasking humankind with the honor and gift of partnering with God in ruling and subduing the earth. Thus there are two parts to the equation. Humans are image-bearers, and are also in partnership with God in his work in the world.

To bear the image of God means that we are created to reflect and represent his heart, character, and righteousness in our lives and also in our interactions with his creation. Being an image-bearer in the biblical story is centered around our mission in the world and how we advance the kingdom of God. It has everything to do not just with who we are but equally with what we were created to do.

As image-bearers, we are meant to partner with God in ruling and subduing the earth. This terminology can have connotations that make us modern people a little uncomfortable, but these connotations are not what the biblical authors had in mind. Context helps a lot. The Lord placed Adam and Eve in a garden. The image here is more of cultivating and caring for what God has initiated—helping achieve his purposes rather than pursuing ours.

It's an active partnership. That is what God has always wanted from his children. In the garden, God didn't want Adam to sit back and watch him work alone. The plan wasn't for Adam to watch God plant the apple tree seed and water it. Or to watch God till the soil and pick the apples when they were ripe while

Adam sat back and sang worship songs. God wanted Adam in the dirt with him caring for what God had started.

Growing up, I always thought that Adam's work began after the fall, but the curse of the fall was the difficulty and burden of work in a fallen world and apart from God. Working with God under his design and purpose has always been a part of God's heart for us.

Then sin entered and shattered the intended relationship between God and humans in the garden. Sin ushered in decay and death and disrupted the ability of humanity to be true image-bearers of God, which prevented them from working with God the way he originally intended. His original purpose, though, did not change. This is the story of the entire Scriptures—God working with and through his people, first through the imperfect nation of Israel and then ultimately through the perfection of Jesus to bring about a new creation and the kingdom of God on earth as it is in heaven. Jesus announced through the gospel that we can join him in his work in the world the way it was meant to be from the beginning. He now calls each of us to join him in proclaiming the message of new life, new creation, and restored purpose as we join him in establishing the kingdom of God in our lives, our families, our relationship, our careers, and our dreams. This purpose isn't limited to one nation or one people group now. It isn't limited to those in professional, full-time ministry. It is for all who have called upon the name of Jesus for salvation and who bear that name. Jesus is the true and perfect image of the invisible God who dwells in us so that we can be image-bearers of God the way we were always meant to be. That is the narrative that our lives as followers of Jesus are brought into.

All of that sounds well and good, but what does it actually mean for my day-to-day life? And for the dreams that God has placed in my heart?

THE GREATEST COMMANDMENT

Jesus showed us what God's purpose means for our daily lives and our dreams when he was questioned by the religious leaders of his day. Even though they could quote the Scriptures better than anyone, they had lost sight of the call to partner *with* God to build his kingdom. Instead, they were using the commandments and Scriptures to build their own. They weren't cultivating God's good creation or the hearts of the people they led; rather, they were subduing people through legalism and religious condemnation.

Here's their exchange with Jesus found in Matthew:

> Hearing that Jesus had silenced the Sadducees, the Pharisees got together. One of them, an expert in the law, tested him with this question: "Teacher, which is the greatest commandment in the Law?"
>
> Jesus replied: "'Love the Lord your God with all your heart and with all your soul and with all your mind.' This is the first and greatest commandment. And the second

is like it: 'Love your neighbor as yourself.' All the Law and the Prophets hang on these two commandments." (Matthew 22:34–40)

Jesus sums up how we are to bear God's image, and the way we are to partner with him in his purpose for the world: by loving God and loving our neighbors. These commandments are a striking contrast to the rules and regulations the religious leaders of the day taught and demanded from the people. The Pharisees had made their lives with God about what they did. But Jesus says following the law is more about *how* you do what you do. He wasn't abolishing the Torah or the commandments; he was pointing to what was underneath it all: a changed heart that produced a changed way of living.

Rather than having to jump through hoops to please God, what if it was more about asking the question, Is God pleased with how I do what I am doing? Is what I am doing loving toward God and loving toward my neighbor?

Sadly, I have fallen into the same trap as the Pharisees time and again in my life and in the pursuit of my dreams or in chasing my ever-elusive "calling." I have made my life about what I do.

What Jesus said in the two greatest commandments, though, isn't contingent on my finding the one right individualized purpose for my life. It's not dependent on writing my own narrative by making my dream a reality. It's not a car phone purpose. It's a portable purpose. It's a matter of carrying the narrative of God's plan with me in all that I do.

Here's how Paul put it in 1 Corinthians 10:31: "So whether you eat or drink or whatever you do, do it all for the glory of God."

Wherever you are in your life, whatever you are doing, God wants to use you for his glory. His glory is your purpose. His glory is meant to be the ultimate narrative of not just creation but your life as well, accomplished through the death and resurrection of Jesus. You are meant to reflect that narrative, which has become your reality, in whatever you are doing. This is what it means to function as an image-bearer—reflecting the love, heart, and grace of Jesus in every interaction. Reflecting his heart in our integrity. In the way we conduct business.

We are image-bearers when we prioritize what God prioritizes by joining him in his creative and redemptive purpose in the world. That can be in creating a new venture, in serving through charitable work, or in simply eating and drinking and enjoying the world he has made.

We must ask ourselves every day, Are we shining a light on the goodness of God in each situation or position we find ourselves in? Are we loving God and loving our neighbor in all things? Doing these things is how we walk in our purpose as redeemed children of God.

I love how Tim Mackie of the Bible Project put it in a podcast I heard recently:

The way that the Bible depicts the purpose of humans is to image God and rule and take the world somewhere on God's behalf as the gift He's granted humanity, and in doing that well through loving God and loving our neighbor humans honor and give glory to God.[1]

This understanding of God's purpose is critical to answering the central question of the book: What is God's purpose for my life? I used to think that my dream was God's purpose for me, and I would wrap the dream up in terms like "calling" to make it sound more spiritual. But a "dream" is different from God's ultimate purpose for one's life. A dream is usually a specific ambition for this life, an ambition to achieve something here on earth, some career, some relationship, or some station in life. It isn't necessarily selfish either. For Christians, God often gives us desires for how we can use our talents and gifts for him, and our dreams often come from these desires.

The danger comes, though, if we think a dream is God's purpose for us, if we confuse a dream with the reason why God created us. A dream may be from God, but it also may not be from him. Or it may be from God for only a season, and then he leads us into a different season, giving us a new dream. When that happens, if we think a particular dream is our purpose, then our whole world and view of our mission on earth can come crashing down. We've lost our spot on the softball field and now we have no cell signal. It's a silly analogy, but when our dreams are threatened or die we may mistakenly think God has abandoned

---

1 Tim Mackie, *God in All Things* podcast. June 22, 2016.

us when in reality his purpose for us has never changed. Only our circumstances have.

Your dreams do not equal your purpose. Your dream is not the destination for your life. It's an avenue that God has given you, but it is not the only way you can achieve your purpose based on what God reveals about purpose in his Word.

THE CLARITY OF A CALLING

But what about this word *calling*? It's a word that gets thrown around all the time if you've grown up in church. You may have heard (or said):

- "I'm called to preach."
- "I'm called to start a business."
- "I'm called to be a wife."
- "I'm called to be a dad."
- "I'm called to be a worship leader and songwriter."

Once we are bold enough to say we are called by God to do something, it becomes pretty difficult for our faith and worldview to stay strong when that thing doesn't come to pass or gets taken away. Could it be that we have misunderstood what the Bible actually says about "calling" too? Or at the least, maybe we have an incomplete view of a calling.

Let's look at a few Scriptures that will help give us perspective as followers of Jesus. First, we are called to salvation through Christ:

Peter replied, "Repent and be baptized, every one of you, in the name of Jesus Christ for the forgiveness of your sins. And you will receive the gift of the Holy Spirit. The promise is for you and your children and for all who are far off—*for all whom the Lord our God will call.*" (Acts 2:38–39, emphasis added)

We are called into relationship with Jesus:

God is faithful, *who has called you into fellowship with his Son*, Jesus Christ our Lord. (1 Corinthians 1:9, emphasis added)

We are called to holiness:

He has saved us and *called us to a holy life*—not because of anything we have done but because of his own purpose and grace. This grace was given us in Christ Jesus before the beginning of time, but it has now been revealed through the appearing of our Savior, Christ Jesus, who has destroyed death and has brought life and immortality to light through the gospel. And of this gospel I was appointed a herald and an apostle and a teacher. (2 Timothy 1:9–11, emphasis added)

We are also called to live in a way that promotes love and unity:

As a prisoner for the Lord, then, I urge you to *live a life worthy of the calling you have received.* Be completely humble and gentle; be patient, bearing with one another in love. Make every effort to keep the unity of the Spirit through the bond of peace. There is one body and one Spirit, just as you were called to one hope when you were called; one Lord, one faith, one baptism; one God and Father of all, who is over all and through all and in all. (Ephesians 4:1–6, emphasis added)

Most of the time in the New Testament, the term *calling* is used more in the context of following Jesus and being in right relationship with him and others than about a career. That's good news for those of you who are still waiting to live out your calling.

You can live out your calling regardless of whether you are living in your dream.

Are some people called for unique assignments? Yes, there are certainly examples in Scripture where someone receives an individual assignment or appointment from God. In the passage above from 2 Timothy 1, in verse 11 Paul says, "And of this gospel I was appointed a herald and an apostle and a teacher." He was appointed by the risen Jesus in a dramatic experience recounted in Acts 9.

The Lord also tells Jeremiah in chapter 1 of his book:

Before I formed you in the womb I knew you,
before you were born I set you apart;

I appointed you as a prophet to the nations. (vv. 4–5)

Not to mention Solomon, who was set apart by God to build the temple instead of David.

And specific assignments weren't reserved just for the apostles and preachers. In Exodus 31 we see another case:

> Then the LORD said to Moses, "See, I have chosen Bezalel son of Uri, the son of Hur, of the tribe of Judah, and I have filled him with the Spirit of God, with wisdom, with understanding, with knowledge and with all kinds of skills—to make artistic designs for work in gold, silver and bronze, to cut and set stones, to work in wood, and to engage in all kinds of crafts. Moreover, I have appointed Oholiab son of Ahisamak, of the tribe of Dan, to help him." (vv. 1–6)

Here Bezalel, a skilled craftsman and artist, who was already honoring God with his work, receives a specific assignment from God. We also see Oholiab appointed as a helper for this specific task.

What I find interesting is that Bezalel was only doing what God had gifted him to do. Bezalel's work likely didn't feel very spiritual. He was just working. He probably learned his skills in Egypt and didn't think there was anything all that spiritual about them. And to him, it probably looked like there wasn't much use for a skilled artist and craftsman as his nation traveled in the wilderness. But the Scripture says that when it came time to build the tabernacle, Bezalel was in a position for God to surprise him and interrupt him with a specific assignment.

Bezalel didn't chase a "calling" to build the tabernacle. He didn't even know that building the tabernacle was on the horizon. But he was faithful to use what he had in each season, and was ready when God tapped him on the shoulder and said, *"This is what I have for you to do right now."*

In fact, as you look at the Scriptures, when people are appointed or assigned by God to do something specific, the assignment is usually unexpected and surprising. It is the result of a Spirit-led encounter initiated by God and usually isn't even on the person's radar. The assignment wasn't the focus of their ambition. Joseph was in an Egyptian prison when he was assigned to lead the nation. David was tending sheep when he was appointed to be a king. Nehemiah was a cupbearer when he began to feel a burden for Jerusalem. Peter, John, and James were fishing when Jesus said, "Follow me." Paul was on his way to put Christians in prison when the Lord appointed him to be an apostle. I like the words *assignment* and *appointment* for these kinds of tasks given by God to his followers because we have misused the word *calling*. None of these assignments were on anyone's ten-year plan. These followers weren't throwing around the word *calling*. But God intervened when there was something specific he wanted them to do.

Here's the point I'm trying to make: It seems that what is most important to God as you look at the totality of the gospel message is that we are called to follow Jesus in whatever we are doing. There is more emphasis on who we are called to follow than on what our own individual calling may or may not be. A calling is not a career path or choice that you chase after, although if you get a specific assignment from God, it may derail your current life trajectory. But you can't chase those assignments. You instead position yourself in a posture of surrender each day in the way you live your live, staying in position for the specific assignments of God that may come by living according to the church-wide calling of living a Christlike life.

The good news is that this kind of life can be lived in any career, in any relationship, and in any location. Your career may be an assignment you have received, but what's most important to understand is that no matter what your career is, you can live out your calling as a Christian right there. You are living out your calling, say, as a fifth-grade teacher no differently and to no lesser degree than as a preacher or a missionary.

We have to change our understanding of "calling" and "purpose" so that they are more in line with the Word of God. If we look again at the example of David, his purpose wasn't to build the temple. It was to be an image-bearer of God and partner with him in what he was doing on earth in order to bring glory to God by loving him and loving his neighbor. David's calling wasn't to build the temple. He was called to live a holy life, conducting his life in a way that honored God and others. He also had a specific assignment given by God as the king of Israel—he was anointed to do that specific task. David's dream, though, was to build a temple. But it was that dream he had to learn to hold loosely.

And so, like David, we need to change our narrative from chasing a calling we wish we had to living out a calling we know we already have.

We need to change our narrative from finding our purpose to living out God's purpose for us wherever we are.

Your purpose is portable, and your calling is too.

This new perspective helps us guard against the pattern we have of making every dream a calling or our purpose. We think any desire we experience points us to God's ultimate design for our life. While I do believe one of the ways God directs us is through our desires, they are but one of the factors we weigh in determining what God is leading us to do. The problem lies in our tendency, or let me say my tendency, to think that my preferred future, that is, my dream, is mandated by God to come about no matter what. While our dreams and desires matter to God, we must always remember that he will never bow to our dreams. Our dreams must instead bow down to Jesus and submit to his purpose and his calling.

PIVOT PRACTICE

Notice your narrative. Write the words *purpose, calling,* and *dreams* on a piece of paper. In the same way that we applied the definitions we learned in this chapter to David's life on page pages 143–144, detail how you would define purpose, calling, and dreams in your own life.

I'll go first:

- **Purpose.** My purpose wasn't to be a worship leader at a particular church. It was and is to be an image-bearer of God and partner with him in what he is doing on the earth in order to bring glory to him by loving God and loving my neighbor.
- **Calling.** My calling wasn't to be a worship leader or a singer or a songwriter, although that was an assignment in a particular season. I am called to live a life of love, holiness, and obedience as a disciple of Jesus. I am called to be a loving and Christlike husband to my wife and father to my daughters. I also believe I have a specific calling to teach, preach, and build the church, which in the past has been lived out through worship

leading, and in this season through speaking and writing.

- **Dreams.** I now have a dream of being an author who teaches through books, podcasting, and coaching, and who preaches in local churches to share the message God has stirred up in my heart in this season. I also have dreams for our family and the life we want to live, but there's not enough room for that here.

Portable purpose. Commit to one way you can live out your purpose each day this week exactly where you are without changing any of your circumstances. It can be one consistent act each day, or seven different actions, one for each day of the week. Share this commitment with a friend at the beginning of the week, and then reconnect at the end to discuss how it made you feel and how you can build on it going forward.

CHAPTER 8

The Calling to Consistency

I have always wanted to be the guy who does great things for God. Not the small acts of faith for "normal" Christians, but gigantic leaps of faith that cause people to take notice. I don't think I'm alone in this either. Just scroll through Instagram and you will find post after post about how you need to do something grand and magnificent in the Lord's name for your life to truly matter.

Many of the voices I listen to internally and externally all preach the same message, and maybe you have started to believe it too. But it's a subtle and very misleading lie. Here's another version of it: My greatest impact happens when I take giant steps of faith.

Maybe you don't struggle with this, but I spend a lot of time thinking that God uses me only when I take a risk, or that I make a difference only when I take a giant step of faith or start some new project for God. I read a study recently that found, on average, people have only fifteen days a year of "perfect" happiness.[1] Two weeks of happiness! I don't know if this is true or not, but I do often feel that in a year I have about two weeks' worth of days in which I'm filled with faith. Fifteen good days of faith a year, and God uses me only when I am in that perfect faith zone, doing incredible things for him. But what about the other fifty weeks of the year, when my days look pretty ordinary? I spend most of my days in meetings and responding to emails, not teaching or writing.

This view of impact, which some of you may share, is particularly deceptive, because it exploits our call as Christians to have faith. Because faith is a good thing, we think that bigger leaps of faith are better, more honoring to God. But this is the truth: My greatest impact doesn't happen through giant steps of faith, but rather through daily steps of faithfulness.

If we are honest, this goes against how we think about our dreams and how we live each day.

You think you will finally have influence and leave your mark

---

1   Ben Renner, "Best. Day. EVER! Survey Finds Average Person Has Only Fifteen 'Perfect' Days a Year," Study Finds, https://www.studyfinds.org/best-day-ever -survey-15-perfect-days-year/.

when you get the opportunity you've been working and praying for. You believe you will make an impact when you have the platform. When you land that dream job or finally reach that financial milestone you've been working toward. When you hit that magic number of followers on IG, which you say you don't really care about but check constantly throughout the day. When your company finally hits that benchmark, then you'll be making a difference.

I admit achieving these things may be momentary wins to celebrate, but are they really what cause your life to have a lasting and significant impact?

Think of the people in your life who have had the most positive and healthy impact on you. Not just for a moment, but people who have made a profound difference in your life. Were they a social media influencer or a famous worship leader? Or were they a parent, brother, sister, friend, teacher, or pastor who was in your life? And someone who was not just present every now and then, but someone who was there consistently.

Consistent.

Can I be honest and admit that I used to hate that word?! I hated it because one thing that people tended to say about me was that I was consistent. You might think that's a good thing, but I thought consistency was boring. And I didn't want to be boring. I wanted people to say that Wade is such a great singer. That he's so smart. That he's got such a quick wit. That he's the life of the party. But instead I got "I really love how consistent you are." That feels the same as "Oh, you've got a great personality." I wanted to be the hot one, not the one with the good personality!

However, one of the things that God celebrates the most in Scripture is consistency. Consistency might not be flashy, but it is powerful. A life well lived, a life that fulfills God's purpose in us and through us, is a life lived consistently. The Bible often calls it steadfastness. First Corinthians 15:58 says: "Therefore, my beloved brothers, be steadfast, immovable, always abounding in the work of the Lord, knowing that in the Lord your labor is not in vain" (ESV).

We get so caught up in the new thing we are excited about, the new step of faith, the new job, we don't realize that God is using us to show the world the power, integrity, and blessing in finishing what we start. There is a blessing when we keep a commitment that is hard. We live in a culture that glorifies moving on when things get hard rather than staying to make something better. So it matters when you honor your word and your commitments. When you push through when it's not easy or stay in the difficult moment when it's the right thing to do, people take notice—because that's not what most people do.

Faith often is less about doing the new thing and more about doing the old thing in a fresh way with a renewed passion. It's about doing the thing that no one notices, the right thing, again and again with a heart to honor God. We like to gravitate toward what is most noticeable. The big step. The huge risk and change. But what I am learning is not to mistake what is most noticeable for what is most valuable.

Consistency isn't flashy. But it is the stuff of marriages that have weathered decades of storms. It is the glue that has kept friendships together through hardship and across continents. It has grown churches and ministries and built businesses conducted with integrity. It has raised children to love God and others. And consistency has passed reform and legislation after decades and even centuries of opposition.

Consistency is what allows you to live out your purpose in any situation, regardless of whether you are living in your dream. It allows you to live a life that makes an impact for the kingdom of God.

Consistency happens one small decision at a time. Small things make a big impact, remember?

A DIFFERENCE IN THE DAILY

Look at Joseph, whose story is told in the final chapters of Genesis. We can't talk about dreams without mentioning Joseph, right? But when I read Joseph's story—how as a teenager he dreamed of greatness, and then his brothers turned against him—I can't find one giant step of faith he took in pursuit of his dream. What I see instead is his consistency in honoring God and living a life of integrity even as his dream seemed further and further out of reach. While he spent many years in slavery and in prison, it was his consistent work ethic and consistent commitment to make the right choices that honored God, who then gave him influence wherever he went. Consistency of character is what allowed Joseph to have the biggest impact.

Joseph was consistent in every season.

You might not be living out your dream, but you can make a difference in the small and often hard things of daily life.

Forgiving someone who betrayed you isn't something most of us feel like doing. But the impact of forgiveness on that person and on your own heart is greater in God's eyes than in achieving most dreams. Defending those in your life who can't defend themselves has a huge impact. Disciplining your kids can be the kindest and most loving thing for them, but it hurts you as a parent. These daily decisions make a huge difference in our world.

In fact, a lot of times chasing a dream can be easier than the small, difficult act of obedience. It's easy to do the things that fulfill our desires—to practice the guitar when you love playing the guitar, to work that job when you find satisfaction in your work, to love that person with whom you want to start a family. Oftentimes we choose our dreams over those small daily acts of obedience—even though those acts of obedience would have a greater impact. And we church up our language and say we have a peace about not doing something. But in reality, sometimes we are backing away from the hard thing and claiming to have peace, when the peace we say that we feel is really relief because we have avoided doing the hard but right thing.

I want to compel you: Don't wait on doing those small, daily things. Not every opportunity lasts forever.

I have been blessed with two amazing parents. Not only did they do an incredible job raising me, but they also are a big part of my life and my kids' lives today. I love my parents a lot. What many people don't know is that technically my dad, Howard, is my stepdad. He began raising me when I was seven and adopted me when I was sixteen. As far as I am concerned, though, he is my real dad.

I haven't seen my biological father since I was four. When I was a baby, I lived in California with him and my mom, and he was basically a white-collar criminal who conned people out of their money. He used cocaine and lived a double life, having countless affairs. After my parents got a divorce, he spent much of my childhood in prison for drugs and money laundering.

About seven years ago I began to feel this pull in my heart to contact my dad and just establish some sort of relationship. I was fairly confident he didn't know the Lord and I thought I was supposed to share Christ with him. But to be honest I was still scared of him. As weird as that sounds as an adult, I had this fear of reaching out. Maybe it was just an aversion to how awkward the interaction would be. So I kept putting it off until I felt better about it, believing the time would eventually be right.

Then one day in October 2016, I got a call from my mom while I was at work saying that my biological dad had passed away. When I heard those words in my office I broke down. Not only grieving for a man I didn't really know, but also broken by the missed chance I had. I let the fear of an awkward conversation prevent me from obeying God and showing his love to my dad. I know I wasn't the only chance he had to hear about Jesus, and I understand God's grace covers my mistakes, but I knew I missed an opportunity I would never get back.

The right thing to do is rarely the path of least resistance.

We think God is calling us to take this huge step but sometimes what he really wants us to do is just make one phone call. One text that can make a big difference. One decision to be there for someone. We end up not obeying God because we think it's not the right time. Or because we don't have the peace. We think it doesn't matter because what God is asking us to do isn't in our eyes a big step of faith. But those little steps, which we can take only by daily surrender to Jesus, can often be the ones that change someone's life.

DAILY PRACTICES

One of the dumbest mistakes I've made occurred a few months before writing this chapter. I was ministering to a church in The Woodlands, Texas, and I needed to be there in person. My wife graciously offered to book my travel one day because I had a full schedule of coaching calls, and so I quickly told her I needed to fly to Dallas because The Woodlands was right outside of Dallas.

Now if you are a Texan, I know you are judging me right now. But for those who aren't familiar with the great state of Texas, I invite you to take out your phone and look on your map app of choice for the nearest major airport to The Woodlands. Spoiler alert: It's not Dallas. In my defense, I knew that The Woodlands was actually outside of Houston, but that's not what came out of my mouth in that moment. So my amazing wife booked the flight to Dallas just like I asked. And neither of us thought about it again until the day of the trip.

Fast-forward several weeks and the moment arrived when I landed in Dallas for my ministry trip to The Woodlands. I got my rental car and looked to see how far away the hotel was, and to my surprise it wasn't thirty minutes away like I expected. It was three and a half hours away! My self-talk the entire drive from Dallas to the outskirts of Houston was not the healthiest, but on the bright side I did get a scenic tour of parts of Texas I had not planned on seeing.

But here's what I thought about as I made that long drive to Houston. The entire flight I had no idea I was headed in the wrong direction. It was the result of a simple, careless decision that led me hundreds of miles away from where I needed to be. But I didn't know I was headed to the wrong destination until I got there. Everything felt normal up to that point.

We can be wildly off course and never even realize it. If we aren't intentional about where we want to go, we might not like where we end up.

Our hearts go in a certain direction, and not in the direction of surrender. To make matters more difficult, oftentimes we don't even realize the direction we're going in because we are moving right in line with the world around us. And so if we're not intentional about where we want to go, we will end up going down the path of least resistance. But in the same way, if we are intentional, we don't have to take big steps.

In James Clear's insightful book *Atomic Habits*, he writes that "habits are how you embody your identity," and "The more you repeat a behavior, the more you reinforce the identity associated with that behavior." Thus, "your habits matter because they help you become the type of person you wish to be."[1]

Our identity as an image-bearer of God is worked out through our daily practices, which in theology is called sanctification. We are saved by grace through faith in Jesus, but it takes a lifetime for our actions to line up with our identity. It takes a lifetime for our character to be conformed to the image of God. And that happens, like James Clear says, through our daily habits and practices. Our consistent spiritual disciplines and practices help us become who we already are in Christ. They form the character of a disciple.

If you want your character to show a pattern of obedience, love, and kindness, you must adopt daily practices of living that reflect those priorities. Your priorities don't become patterns until you start to adopt small practices. And those practices must be acted on consistently for real change to occur.

We talked earlier about how small lies can corrupt an entire belief system. Yet here is where the principle behind that truth works in our favor: Small practices repeated over time lead to massive change. The small acts of obedience help us form patterns in our lives and those patterns, over time, change and shape our character. And even though ultimately it is the Holy Spirit's job to transform our hearts and help us obey, we must practice our faith daily.

---

1   James Clear, *Atomic Habits: An Easy & Proven Way to Build Good Habits & Break Bad Ones* (New York: Avery, 2018), 36–37, 41.

Many of us don't like to hear that we actually need to take action in our faith. We tend to say that daily practices of faith or disciplines sound legalistic. But discipline is not the same as legalism. Legalism is born out of a spirit of performance and trying to earn favor or look good in the eyes of God or others. Discipline is building your life around your priorities and passion. A life of discipline becomes a life of transformation.

Let us look again at David. His response to God's *"No"*—David's trust in God's goodness and plan—I assure you was not a knee-jerk reaction. It was the response of a heart and character shaped by God. While we don't have access to David's daily schedule, we do have many of his daily prayers in the Psalms, and these prayers, as well as the stories we do have about David, give us insight into the daily spiritual life of the man after God's own heart. In fact, in these prayers and stories, we see evidence of four disciplines in David's life that helped form his character and, importantly, his willingness to surrender.

CONSISTENT CONTEMPLATION ON GOD

David is credited with writing 73 of the 150 psalms in Scripture. These psalms aren't full of churchy platitudes. They are brutally honest. They express magnificent joy and praise to God right alongside crushing laments of despair and disappointment. The entire emotional spectrum is on display in David's prayer journal, and throughout it all, we see a man who is devoted to focusing his heart on the Lord even in his disappointment.

Much has been written about David's authenticity in these

This Dream Is Not for You

prayers, but the specific aspect I want to highlight is what they show about the frequency of David's contemplation of God:

> Listen to my voice in the morning, LORD. *Each morning I bring my requests to you* and wait expectantly. (Psalm 5:3 NLT, emphasis added)

> As for me, I will call upon God, and the LORD shall save me. *Evening and morning and at noon* I will pray, and cry aloud, and He shall hear my voice. (Psalm 55:16–17 NKJV, emphasis added)

> *Every day I call to you*, my God, but you do not answer. *Every night I lift my voice*, but I find no relief. (Psalm 22:2 NLT, emphasis added)

David didn't just pray and focus his heart on the Lord when he felt like it. He prioritized his life around a rhythm of prayer and contemplation. He prayed even when he couldn't sense an answer from the Lord. And we see this same practice and instruction in the New Testament. Paul calls believers to consistent prayer:

> Rejoice always, *pray continually*, give thanks in all circumstances; for this is God's will for you in Christ Jesus. (1 Thessalonians 5:16–18, emphasis added)

Praying at all times in the Spirit, with all prayer and supplication. To that end, keep alert with all perseverance, making supplication for all the saints. (Ephesians 6:18 ESV)

Since, then, you have been raised with Christ, *set your hearts on things above*, where Christ is, seated at the right hand of God. *Set your minds on things above*, not on earthly things. (Colossians 3:1–2)

Jesus also demonstrates his practice of prioritizing prayer in the middle of a very overwhelming ministry schedule:

Very early in the morning, while it was still dark, Jesus got up, left the house and went off to a solitary place, where he prayed. (Mark 1:35)

Simply put, being a disciple is being a person of prayer. That doesn't mean a one-way conversation either. A healthy conversation involves vulnerability to share, as well as proper and authentic humility to listen. It's in prayer that we tell God our dreams, and it is in prayer that we also surrender them as we discern what the Holy Spirit wants to say to us through Scripture. Prayer is one of the main ways we gain new wisdom from the Lord regarding what to pursue or what to lay down. It's where we feel the conviction and comfort of the Holy Spirit.

I believe it was from David's prayers, which he prayed

throughout his day, that allowed him to have the heart to surrender his dream of building a temple to the Lord. Similarly, it was Daniel's rhythm of praying three times a day in Babylonian exile that gave him strength and the courage to stand up to persecution (see Dan. 6:10).

Likewise, it was Jesus' dependence on the Father through prayer that allowed him to pivot in his most vulnerable hour and say:

> Father, if you are willing, take this cup from me; yet not my will, but yours be done. (Luke 22:42)

A life of prayer becomes a life of surrender. And instead of dreaming each day, we, like David, should set our hearts on God and his plans and purposes.

CONSISTENT CHARACTER IN THE COMMONPLACE

The very first time we meet David in the Scriptures, we are introduced to a shepherd, not a king. While the rest of his brothers are lined up before a prophet chasing status, David is faithfully doing his duty as a lowly shepherd.

> So [Samuel] asked Jesse, "Are these all the sons you have?" "There is still the youngest," Jesse answered. "He is tending the sheep." (1 Samuel 16:11)

Continuing into the next few verses, we see the prophet Samuel anoint David as king of Israel:

> Samuel said, "Send for him; we will not sit down until he arrives." So he sent for him and had him brought in. He was glowing with health and had a fine appearance and handsome features. Then the LORD said, "Rise and anoint him; this is the one." So Samuel took the horn of oil and anointed him in the presence of his brothers, and from that day on the Spirit of the LORD came powerfully upon David. Samuel then went to Ramah. (vv. 11–13)

You would think that as soon as David received this assignment from Samuel he would immediately abandon any task he deemed beneath a king. Yet he did not. In fact, David spends the next fifteen years not reigning as king but instead doing common duties. For example, we learn later, in verse 19, that after being anointed David returned to the flock. He returned to his ordinary life. Later, when no one else in the nation would stand up to the Philistines and their giant Goliath, David did his duty for God and his nation. But David had the strength to fight this particular battle because of what he learned in his common service to his family as a shepherd:

> "The LORD who rescued me from the paw of the lion and the paw of the bear will rescue me from the hand of this

Philistine." Saul said to David, "Go, and the LORD be with you." (1 Samuel 17:37)

When Saul, the king whom David was destined to replace, needed someone to care for his equipment, David said yes. When Saul needed a soldier, David did his duty and went to battle. When Saul needed a musician to soothe his troubled spirit, David played his lyre—even though Saul tried to kill him with a spear. And when David finally had to run from Saul and leave behind his friends and family to save his own life, David didn't mount an insurrection. Instead, he became the protector and leader of a band of misfits and outcasts. People just like him.

While on the run from Saul, we learn that:

David left Gath and escaped to the cave of Adullam. When his brothers and his father's household heard about it, they went down to him there. All those who were in distress or in debt or discontented gathered around him, and he became their commander. About four hundred men were with him. (1 Samuel 22:1–2)

David cared for the common people. There was something about David that drew those that were hurting to him. He didn't run from the mess of the ordinary. He embraced where he was, in a hidden and dirty cave, with broken and looked-over people, to live out his purpose and do good even when he was not celebrated by the masses. He helped the people he could help in the moment, rather than waiting for a platform to finally do good.

David also refused to take matters into his own hands, and he refused to manipulate outcomes that would have fast-tracked him in his assignment. He didn't try to take shortcuts to power or success when it wasn't God's timing. This is especially on display when David had a chance to kill Saul when Saul went to relieve himself alone in a cave, the same cave that David was hiding in. In that moment, David could have ended Saul's life and taken his rightful place as king. He could have told God he was tired of the common life and was ready to claim what was meant to be his. The kingship was within his grasp, but David knew it wasn't his to take. It was God's gift to give.

Then David went out of the cave and called out to Saul, "My lord the king!" When Saul looked behind him, David bowed down and prostrated himself with his face to the ground. He said to Saul, "Why do you listen when men say, 'David is bent on harming you'? This day you have seen with your own eyes how the LORD delivered you into my hands in the cave. Some urged me to kill you, but I spared you; I said, 'I will not lay my hand on my lord, because he is the LORD's anointed.' See, my father, look at this piece of your robe in my hand! I cut off the corner of your robe but did not kill you. See that there is nothing in my hand to indicate that I am guilty of wrongdoing or rebellion. I have not wronged you, but you are hunting me down to take my life. May the LORD judge between you and me. And may the LORD avenge the wrongs you have done to me, but my hand will not touch you." (1 Samuel 24:8–12)

David showed the character to serve well in what everyone else would have perceived as commonplace, and in doing so he lived a life of purpose even though he was not yet living out his assignment to be king. He demonstrated a deep trust in the truth that God was in charge of the ultimate outcome of his life.

Paul instructs the church in Thessalonica to do the same:

Now about your love for one another we do not need to write to you, for you yourselves have been taught by God to love each other. And in fact, you do love all of God's family throughout Macedonia. Yet we urge you, brothers and sisters, to do so more and more, and to make it your ambition to lead a quiet life: You should mind your own business and work with your hands, just as we told you, so that your daily life may win the respect of outsiders and so that you will not be dependent on anybody. (1 Thessalonians 4:9–12)

This is also wisdom for any dreamer. Do not despise the commonplace, for it is in the quiet moments of life that your love and character often speak the loudest.

CONSISTENT COMMITMENT TO GOD'S HOUSE

At his core David was a worshipper. His words in the Psalms became a significant part of Israel's prayer and worship liturgy, as they are two thousand years later for the church. David didn't confine his worship to his private prayers—he was equally passionate about the public worship of Yahweh.

In Psalm 69:9, David expresses his passion for the house of God: "For zeal for your house consumes me." And we see the evidence of that zeal throughout his entire life, whether in his care in transporting the ark to Jerusalem or his dream to build the temple as a permanent house for God.

Throughout the Psalms David admonishes us to gather in corporate worship and bring God praise, exaltation, and thanksgiving. He continually declares his intention to bring God public praise: "I will declare your name to my people; in the assembly I will praise you" (Ps. 22:22).

Worship isn't passive for David. It isn't about what he receives. It is about what he can bring. Corporate worship is an opportunity for the people of God to come to the Lord with hearts that are open.

This is especially evident in the New Testament. We see that gathering together as followers of Jesus is crucial for Christian life and a chief catalyst for the gospel to go forth:

Let us hold unswervingly to the hope we profess, for he who promised is faithful. And let us consider how we may spur one another on toward love and good deeds, not giving up meeting together, as some are in the habit of doing, but encouraging one another—and all the more as you see the Day approaching. (Hebrews 10:23–25)

Every day they continued to meet together in the temple courts. They broke bread in their homes and ate together with glad and sincere hearts, praising God and enjoying the favor of all the people. And the Lord added to their number daily those who were being saved. (Acts 2:46–47)

You cannot pursue a dream faithfully and not be rooted in a community of believers through the local church. A dream not planted in the local community of Jesus is like a tree without roots. You are missing your support structure and nourishment. As a believer, and as a dreamer, you are activated and commissioned in your purpose as you worship together with other followers in the house of God.

CONSISTENT CONFESSION OF SIN

Despite all that we have said so far about David's character, no one can argue that he was perfect. In fact, he was far from it, especially in his later years. You can speculate that as he became more and more successful as a king, he grew complacent and perhaps no longer practiced his disciplines of faith. We of course don't know. But we do know that he committed adultery and murder, he was an absentee father, and he disobeyed the Lord in performing a census when he shouldn't have. It wasn't pretty.

Yet, even though he committed those sins, David is still referred to in the New Testament as a man after God's own heart (see Acts 13:22). How can that be?

I believe the answer is found in David's ability to practice the most important discipline, repentance and the confession of sin.

In every instance recorded in Scripture where we find that David sinned against the Lord, we also see evidence of his confession of that sin to God and others. His heart, though not perfect, always threw itself before the mercy of the Lord in confession, and often in desperation and dependency.

When David is confronted by the prophet Nathan about his sin of adultery and murder in 2 Samuel 12:13, David confesses: "Then David said to Nathan, 'I have sinned against the LORD.' Nathan replied, 'The LORD has taken away your sin. You are not going to die.'"

David's private prayer of repentance becomes a public prayer for his people to follow in Psalm 51:

> Have mercy on me, O God, according to your unfailing
>   love;
> according to your great compassion blot out my
>   transgressions.
> Wash away all my iniquity and cleanse me from my sin.
> For I know my transgressions, and my sin is always
>   before me.

Against you, you only, have I sinned and done what is evil in your sight. (vv. 1–4)

On one occasion David was so busy mourning the death of his son Absalom, who had just tried to overthrow and kill his own father, that David abandoned his leadership responsibilities to the people who had fought for him and protected his kingdom:

Then Joab went into the house to the king and said, "Today you have humiliated all your men, who have just saved your life and the lives of your sons and daughters and the lives of your wives and concubines. You love those who hate you and hate those who love you. You have made it clear today that the commanders and their men mean nothing to you. I see that you would be pleased if Absalom were alive today and all of us were dead. Now go out and encourage your men. I swear by the LORD that if you don't go out, not a man will be left with you by night-fall. This will be worse for you than all the calamities that have come on you from your youth till now."

So the king got up and took his seat in the gateway. When the men were told, "The king is sitting in the gateway," they all came before him. (2 Samuel 19:5–8, emphasis added)

David was confronted by Joab and then was humble enough to change course.

We see another example after David disobeyed the Lord by taking a census of his fighting men, which showed a lack of trust in God:

> David was conscience-stricken after he had counted the fighting men, and he said to the LORD, "I have sinned greatly in what I have done. Now, LORD, I beg you, take away the guilt of your servant. I have done a very foolish thing." (2 Samuel 24:10)

Repentance isn't a practice we can abandon either once we receive the grace of Jesus. While the sins of those in Christ are paid once and for all, we are still called to humble ourselves before God and others and acknowledge our sin when we become aware of it, and then turn from that sin as we change our actions and renew our mindsets. In the book of 1 John we see that repentance and confession isn't optional, it is necessary as a disciple:

> If we claim to be without sin, we deceive ourselves and the truth is not in us. If we confess our sins, he is faithful and just and will forgive us our sins and purify us from all unrighteousness. If we claim we have not sinned, we make him out to be a liar and his word is not in us. (1:8–10)

You will never be able to surrender your dreams to God if you can't ever admit that you are wrong or in need of God's grace.

In contrast, it is when you humble yourself before God, and are open enough to accept correction from others, that you gain the much-needed peace, clarity, wisdom, and freedom that come only on the other side of confession.

PIVOT PRACTICE

- **My greatest impact doesn't happen through giant steps of faith, but rather through daily steps of faithfulness.** What small responsibility in your life have you been looking down on that is actually the building block for something God is forming in you? Identify it and thank him for it now. Pray for the strength to be faithful.
- **Consistency practice.** Of the four practices that produce the character of a disciple, in which one do you need to become more disciplined? What steps will you take this week to do so?
  - Consistent contemplation on God
  - Consistent character in the commonplace
  - Consistent commitment to God's house
  - Consistent confession of sin

PART IV

Run Your Race

CHAPTER 9

Don't Give Up on Your Race

I've experienced more than one this-dream-is-not-for-you moment in my life. While I've focused in this book primarily on my dead dream of being a worship leader, another dream died about twenty years earlier. In fact, I had forgotten about it until I was encouraged to transition away from leading worship at Elevation.

I've already recounted the incredible success of the Wade Joye Band. That is, if by success you mean I was working the South Carolina Christian youth camp and retreat circuit and spending whatever offering was given to me on repairs to my white van affectionately known as Blizzie (named accordingly after one harrowing trip in a snowstorm to Arkansas).

My dream in those days was to be a Christian recording artist. I wanted to have my name on the cover of *CCM Magazine*, right there with the great Steven Curtis Chapman. In fact, I learned how to play guitar from listening to Steven Curtis Chapman tapes—I can still sing every lyric of "The Great Adventure" on command. During that time I wrote, recorded, and performed my songs. It would have of course been really nice if I sold a lot of CDs along the way, but at heart I did want to serve God through ministry and use my gifts and passion for music celebrating his kingdom. I had many role models, like Steven Curtis Chapman, who had an incredibly fruitful ministry. I wanted to be like them, and I prayed that one day I could write a song that the world would sing. That became my big, crazy prayer over the years.

In college, though, I began to notice a tug-of-war in my heart. When I was booked for a camp or retreat, I would often lead worship for several sessions, and then as part of the event I would also do a show of my own music. I hate to admit this now, but at the time I thought of the worship sets as something I had to do in order to do what I really loved. I would push through leading worship so I could live out my CCM rock star dream during the final Saturday night concert of the Disciple Now Weekend at some First Baptist Church in South Carolina. I wanted people to love and sing my songs, not lead people in singing someone else's songs.

However, I soon noticed something that I tried to reason

away. When I performed a concert, people seemed to enjoy it but nothing truly special happened beyond a little bit of singing and some praise from the audience. This is not to say that when others perform their music for a group nothing special happens, but there was something missing when *I* did it. When I led worship, though, that's when I began to see God move, and I realized I was good at it. What's more, I realized that I had some measure of gifting and anointing for it. Other people started to affirm this in me, and I began to get booked way more for leading worship than anything else. It was hard for me to deny that God was blessing this aspect of ministry more than my own songwriting.

The problem was that leading worship wasn't "the dream." As a result, I continued to fight it and pursue my own ambitions to be an artist. This led me to attend a Gospel Music Association event in Nashville. I thought if I was going to make it in Christian music, this was where it would happen. This was my shot. I had every expectation that I would leave that week with a recording contract and publishing deal in hand, and I'd be on my way to becoming best friends with Michael W. Smith.

Things didn't quite work out that way, and after one particularly discouraging day at the GMA, I was up late praying and having a psalm-of-lament moment with God. I wondered why he would give me this dream only to shut every door in my face. After I had poured out all of my frustration and emptied myself of tears, I felt the clear voice of the Holy Spirit in my heart:

"I'm going to take you there, but not this way."

I tried to reason with the Lord, telling him that there was no way to get there but this way. All roads to become a Christian recording artist led to Nashville and through the Gospel Music Association.

"I'm going to take you there, but not this way."

This refrain in my spirit wasn't going away. While I didn't like it, I really did want to trust God. This moment did prove pivotal in my life because from then on I decided to surrender that dream to God. The Striving Self was only leaving me frustrated. It was time to live out of the Surrendered Self in obedience and trust. I didn't give it up all at once, but I did make one key decision. I wanted to be open to something that wasn't in my plan. If God really was blessing me when I led worship, I needed to lean in and explore that.

Nothing immediately changed in my position in life, but something significantly changed in the posture of my heart. I began to embrace my gifting as a worship leader, something that wasn't on my radar years ago and that I had fought against. I even went on staff at a local Methodist church as a youth pastor and worship leader for three years before Elevation. It was at that Methodist church that I truly fell in love with the local church, even if the "contemporary service" was a far cry from the loud guitars of the Wade Joye Band. My love for leading worship, pastoring high school students in youth groups, and serving

God's people in the local church laid the foundation for what God eventually led me to do at Elevation.

Twenty years, give or take, after that word from God in a Nashville hotel, I was faced with another word from the Lord that I couldn't reason away or deny. The this-is-not-for-you moment at Elevation sounded pretty similar to the *"not this way"* that I heard years before in Nashville. Yet it was the memory of what God spoke two decades earlier, and retracing the steps since that decision to trust him, that led me to an eye-opening revelation. I was standing in the dream that I thought had died in Nashville. I was hearing a *"No"* to my current dream of being a worship leader while standing in the middle of the dream I thought had died years ago.

Not every no is forever.

In that hotel room, I couldn't have imagined that two decades later I would help serve and lead at a church that would transform the way worship was done in the contemporary church and impact countless lives. No way I could have known that we would write and release songs that would be used in worship all over the world. How could I have imagined that I would get to be a part of writing songs that would be sung in praise to Jesus not only at concerts, but in churches on other continents?

God had brought that dream to pass without my having to chase it. The dream was fulfilled not because of my striving, but through my surrender to God's plan. It happened when I stopped chasing and became open to go wherever God led. Therefore, on that day in my room, after being encouraged to step away from my role of leading worship at Elevation, God didn't need to write it in the sky that he would be faithful. I knew I could trust him as I laid down this dream, just like in that Nashville hotel room. I would be open to a new dream from God.

I wonder if David had a similar experience when God told him that Solomon would build the temple. As David processed that *"No"* and the resulting disappointment, did he realize that he was standing in the middle of the kingdom God had promised him as a teenager? Did he recall that after receiving the promise, he didn't take up a crown, but instead would return to shepherding, face Goliath, and spend years as a fugitive? The path marked out for him to become king was full of opposition—whether in delays or closed doors. Yet God was faithful, and he asked David to trust him again.

We explored earlier how we can't let the dream define us, but we also must be careful to not define prematurely the dream itself. Trusting God with a dream requires just that—trust. When David was being hunted by Saul, he didn't know if he would be killed by Saul and not become king. All he had to hang on to was what God said to him about his assignment. And even that word came through Samuel—it was not an audible voice from God that David heard with his own ears. There had to be moments when David wondered if his assignment was even real.

Most of us haven't experienced an audible voice from God, telling us God's plan for our lives. We do our best to pray and discern, but there is always an element of wonder and the unknown.

EYE ON THE PRIZE

I resonate with how the apostle Paul and the author of Hebrews frame our life as a race. I don't have a love of running or anything—I'm done by around mile 2. But I'm fascinated by extreme races and ultramarathons, and by the people who run them. I'm amazed that for some people, running a hundred-mile race is their dream. The terrain is hard, the weather conditions are tough, and you can't see the first checkpoint for miles, much less the finish line, which can take days to reach. How do these runners do it? What gives them the willpower, strength, and endurance to finish—to discipline their minds, emotions, and bodies to keep going against all odds?

Here's what Paul teaches about racing in 1 Corinthians 9:

> Do you not know that in a race all the runners run, but only one gets the prize? Run in such a way as to get the prize. Everyone who competes in the games goes into strict training. They do it to get a crown that will not last, but we do it to get a crown that will last forever. (vv. 24–25)

The discipline needed for a race is connected to the prize at the end. That is, what you are willing to endure is tied to the value of the prize. And this is true today. The prizes for many of these ultramarathons are beautiful medals or substantial amounts of money. And for many professional racers, the prize is more than the medal and more than the money. The prize may be the respect of peers, or proving to themselves that they can do something most people can't. Whatever it is, there is something in their mind's eye that is drawing them to the finish line, and what that thing is will determine whether they press on or quit in the face of pain and unforeseen difficulty.

No matter how great the prize is for any race on this earth, the prize is temporary. No matter how good the reward is, it doesn't last. The medals gather dust. The money will be spent. The respect will need to be earned again after a new record is set. It is all fleeting, and at some point every runner will retire when the prizes aren't worth it anymore or when their body gives out.

Paul is telling us, however, that the race we are running has the greatest prize—not a medal or money, but a crown and one that lasts forever. (I have yet to see a coronation at a finish line, but I'd love to!)

It might be the case that some of you wouldn't be that interested in getting a literal crown, even an eternal one. But the author of Hebrews adds to this image of a race and our prize:

> Therefore, since we are surrounded by such a great cloud of witnesses, let us throw off everything that hinders and the sin that so easily entangles. And let us run with perseverance the race marked out for us, fixing our eyes on Jesus, the pioneer and perfecter of faith. For the joy set before him he endured the cross, scorning its shame, and sat down at the right hand of the throne of God. Consider

him who endured such opposition from sinners, so that you will not grow weary and lose heart. (12:1–3)

The author doesn't say, "And let us run with perseverance the race marked out for us, fixing our eyes on our *dream*." But all too often that's exactly how I live. I can't overstate the danger of this approach to life and the damage it has done to me. If the dream is my prize, and the dream is lost or in jeopardy, then why run at all? Why work, why endure?

No, the author of Hebrews tells us to fix our eyes on Jesus. The dream isn't the destination. It's not the goal. It never can be. Nor is a literal crown. Jesus is the prize. Knowing him. Loving him. Being in his presence. Bringing glory to him through our lives.

I used to think this idea of receiving Jesus as the prize was such a churchy answer, but the older I get and the more I run my race, I've realized that nothing else truly satisfies. I've achieved many dreams, while many dreams continue to be out of reach. But what I've seen through it all is that nothing fulfills and satisfies the deepest parts of my soul but Christ.

Your dream may be part of your race. It may be a portion of the route marked out for you. In fact, there may be different dreams for different miles of your race. But your dreams must facilitate your purpose—magnifying Christ and bringing the reality of the new creation of Jesus to every corner of our world.

Christ is the prize, and as a child of God you already have

this reward. We don't arrive one day and finally get Christ. We already have Christ in us, the hope of glory. What we will get more of, however, is the joy of knowing him on a deeper level and experiencing him in greater fullness in the new creation. It will be the joy of seeing the fruit of his grace working through our obedience and even bringing about some good through our failures.

THE RACE MARKED OUT FOR US

Even with your eye on the prize, it doesn't mean the race will be easy. Some miles will be smooth. Some may even lead you to your dream. Others will be difficult, full of trials. These are the miles you have to run that you never would have chosen for the race.

This is where I get tripped up in my own race. I wish the markers were set out just a little differently. Sometimes I wish I could alter my gifts, my background, and my opportunities. I would choose to change legs of the race that seem to bring only pain and frustration. I wish I could adjust my own limitations. Being a little taller would be at the top of that list, but I've had to accept that many of my markers can't be changed. We may be able to work to position ourselves for better opportunities, but many times we can't. Often, the markers are out of our control. There are facts that we have to face.

Some markers are set as soon as we are born. We don't choose our family. We don't choose the country or the socioeconomic status we are born into. We don't choose our race or gender, which, unfortunately, often determines the degree of opportunity that is readily available to us. There are health conditions that we have no control over.

In my daughter Sydney's life, there is nothing we can do to change the markers of her race, which include cystic fibrosis. Yes, we pray and believe for healing. We seek all the medical treatment she can get. But her genetic condition is a part of her race that she cannot control.

Part of our race is marked out for us based on our giftings and assignments from God. But also I've learned that God gives us some freedom to set some markers for ourselves and to be creative with different routes. There is a lot of room to run in the kingdom, but there are some markers that we just can't move.

This is the crux of what I want us to wrestle with in the final chapters of the book. How do we know whether an obstacle in our race is telling us to abandon the path we are on and take another path, perhaps take up another dream?

When faced with opposition, the questions we ask ourselves can become endless. When I get derailed and am back at square one, does that mean it's time to give up? Or do I just run harder? Is God stopping me or trying to derail me? Is this obstacle a delay or the death of my dream? Of course, the line between a death and a delay can be extremely thin—how can I know which side of the line I'm on?

These are questions we all face, and I'm not sure we can really know the answers with certainty, in this life anyway. There is no way for me or anyone to tell you what God is purposing in each moment of your life and how it is setting you up for the next leg of your race.

I'm not able to tell you if God is calling you to give up on your dream or whether it's just delayed, or if he has a different dream for you. It's also possible that your dead dream will be resurrected in a future leg of the race. Only God knows the full route of the race. But one thing I know is that a dead dream doesn't mean your race is over. We can learn how to run our race even if we don't know where each mile will take us or what dreams we'll achieve along the way.

The point is that we need to keep running, and not let opposition, whether in the form of delay, defeat, or discouragement, keep us from running our race.

So don't give up on your race.

The author of Hebrews, when encouraging us to run and persevere, also tells us to consider the example of Christ, so let's do that for a moment. The race marked out before Jesus was full of trials and it ultimately led to the cross. And as we know from Jesus' prayer in the Garden of Gethsemane, he asked his Father if there was a different path he could run. Yet even though he asked this of his Father, he made himself obedient to the will of his Father, which meant his death. But it was because of "the joy set before him he endured the cross" (Heb. 12:2).

When we are running and we question our dreams, God's will, or where we're going, if we consider Christ and how he ran, we may not find the answers, but we learn how to run—how to persevere in delay, defeat, and discouragement.

IN DELAY, WHAT CAN I DEVELOP?

As we look at the example of Jesus, we see that after his baptism, which initiated his ministry, he was led by the Spirit into the wilderness for forty days of fasting, prayer, and testing. This of course delayed his ministry. But during this time Jesus was being prepared for his work and ultimately for his death on the cross. In resisting the temptations of the flesh, the eyes, and the pride of life, he was developing the perfect obedience, which he would display throughout the next three years of his earthly ministry.

A delay in your dream gives you the chance to develop a skill needed to achieve the dream. One of our musicians on the Elevation Worship team is named Dom, and he's a key member of the team. He plays most weekends, has recorded on our albums as well as for other artists, and has toured all over the world. But before any of that happened he dreamed of playing for Elevation Worship and auditioned twice. That's because the first time he didn't make it. After the first audition, he was told why and given some direction on what he could work on. He wanted it badly enough that he practiced diligently until the next audition came around. He took the rejection not as a rejection of him or his dream, but rather as an indication that he needed more development.

There are also times when we feel we've reached the limit of what we can do to advance a dream. We're working hard and developing skills—we're doing everything in our control. When this happens, we can always work on ourselves, our character.

First and foremost we can ask ourselves, *How is the Lord wanting me to grow in my trust? In my patience?*

Or is there something in my life that has become the prize more than Jesus? Am I motivated more by selfish ambition and need to grow in championing others by celebrating their opportunities? Does the way I feel about this delay bring to mind someone I need to have a conversation with because I have placed them in a similar position of feeling aimless and confused?

Indeed, when it comes to my character, there are a lot of possibilities for improvement. Though it's easier to skip these hills in the race and just run downhill, it's during these climbs that character is developed. These aspects of our hearts may need to be strengthened for the miles ahead, and it's in the waiting season that God gives us an opportunity for that growth.

IN DEFEAT, WHAT CAN I DISCOVER?

Jesus experienced the ultimate defeat, at least from a human point of view, when he was crucified on the cross. His resurrection, though, became the first fruit of God's new creation. His seeming "defeat" was actually the defeat of his enemies, including death itself.

Jesus' whole ministry was a journey of discovery as he taught and demonstrated that the kingdom of God was not what people thought it was. He turned religious expectations and long-held assumptions on their head when he came as a suffering servant, not as a violent usurper of power who sought to liberate political Israel. He called the overlooked and forgotten, those who didn't think they could dream of being used by God, and birthed the kingdom in their hearts and lives while the religious leaders missed it. Jesus was doing a new thing, and it came first to those who thought they were defeated and without hope.

Some of the greatest times of self-discovery for me have been in the wake of what looked like failure. In the middle of what I considered defeat, I more often than not discovered some of the most important truths about trusting God and becoming aware of a gift he had put in me.

My dream of being a Christian singer and songwriter seemed over when I felt God tell me he would take me a different way. At that moment, I had no idea he would put inside me a great love for the local church. Or that I would be a worship pastor who would write worship songs. Or that I would get to teach and preach at my favorite church on the planet. None of this was on my radar. I couldn't see far enough ahead to know that these things were marked out for me in my race. I discovered them only when I took steps of obedience and trust, one step at a time.

David writes in Psalm 37,

The LORD directs the steps of the godly.
He delights in every detail of their lives. (v. 23 NLT)

Earlier in life, when I read this verse, it meant to me that God would direct my steps by showing me where to go, which would result in my taking steps toward that destination. But now that I can look back on significant portions of my life, I've discovered that God directs me as I take a step, not while I am standing still. It's in doing the next right thing in front of me that I discover his guidance. I am learning to trust that if I am seeking God, even if I take a wrong step, he will redirect me as long as I just keep moving.

We also have to be willing to discover new things along the way. That's when discovery happens—on the journey. We can't judge what God will do in mile 20 by what we are experiencing in mile 2. In all of our lives there are dreams that God gives us at certain stages, dreams we haven't even imagined yet. As we run, we discover gifts, talents, and passions only at the opportune time. Many times, those discoveries happen as a result of the opposition and defeat we face.

In the years since I made my transition from worship leader to more of a pastor, I have discovered several new passions and gifts, chief of which is a new love for studying and teaching God's Word, both in preaching and in writing. This book wasn't on my dream list five years ago. It's a new dream I discovered on the other side of a no.

God's dream for David far exceeded the dream David had for the temple. Remember, God wanted to use David to build a house through which the Messiah would be born. That wasn't on David's agenda, but it was on God's. Leave room for God to truly do more than you can imagine.

And when you are facing defeat, take heart that it's a signal to get ready. To be open to the new thing God wants to bring to your attention. You may discover there's more in you and more going on around you than you ever could have imagined.

IN DISCOURAGEMENT, WHAT CAN I DISPLAY?

A dream usually dies at the hands of others. It feels personal. It seems like an attack or a rejection of who we are, especially if we are defined by the dream. Even when we have the right perspective, though, it still hurts, no matter who we are. And it's in those moments that my reaction is not the most righteous. I get bitter. I root for other people to fail. I get easily offended and discouraged.

Let's one more time consider Christ:

> Do nothing out of selfish ambition or vain conceit. Rather, in humility value others above yourselves, not looking to your own interests but each of you to the interests of the others. In your relationships with one another, have the same mindset as Christ Jesus:
> Who, being in very nature God,
> did not consider equality with God something to be used
> to his own advantage;
> rather, he made himself nothing
> by taking the very nature of a servant,
> being made in human likeness.
> And being found in appearance as a man,
> he humbled himself

by becoming obedient to death—
even death on a cross!
Therefore God exalted him to the highest place
and gave him the name that is above every name,
that at the name of Jesus every knee should bow,
in heaven and on earth and under the earth,
and every tongue acknowledge that Jesus Christ is Lord,
to the glory of God the Father. (Philippians 2:3–11)

Have you been rejected? Christ was rejected by those he made and came to save.

Have you had to serve in a position you thought was beneath you? The Creator came to serve those he created.

Have you had to endure unjust treatment? Jesus was mocked, beaten, and condemned to death, yet he humbled himself out of obedience.

Have you given up wealth, privilege, or status for the sake of obeying God? Jesus did not consider his power something to use for his advantage.

Have you experienced pain and heartbreak? Jesus came in human likeness to live in our weakness, even to the point of death. Yet it was through this suffering and death that Christ displayed the power of God through the resurrection and his exaltation.

In the same way, we are called to model a life that values service more than status, and by doing this we stand out from the world. This is how we shine as stars in the universe in a culture blinded by the darkness of selling out in the name of selfish ambition.

This kind of life and love is not natural. When it's displayed, people take notice. And this type of love is seen clearest when we are in the middle of our frustration, discouragement, and disappointment. Oftentimes God grants us our greatest impact on others when we respond to rejection lovingly and graciously.

In discouragement, consider Christ. Choose to put the character of Christ on display, and keep running.

PIVOT PRACTICE

Meditate on the three questions we explored in this chapter:

- In delay, what can I develop?
- In defeat, what can I discover?
- In discouragement, what can I display?

Take a moment to answer each of them. Pick one to focus on and attach an action step that you can take this week.

CHAPTER 10

Guard Your Gratitude

Several years ago I threw an epic party for my twins' eighth birthday, and it was great—they were running all over the place, playing with their friends and fueled by an ungodly amount of sugar. But while they were having the time of their lives, I was at a different party. Though, yes, I was a chaperone at their party, and I watched them play from my back deck, I was also having a pity party. I tend to have these at times. I always accept the invite, and then realize I'm the only one who RSVP'd.

This particular pity party resulted from watching all the kids run around in my backyard and noticing that Liana was strug-gling to keep up. She was falling behind her friends because of the weakness in her right leg and her leg brace, both a result of the brain bleed when she was born. Her slower pace was barely noticeable to others, but I knew that it hurt her to run, and my father's heart hurt for her. I started asking the questions that often play on repeat in my head. *Why does she have to have this disability? Why can't she do the things Adleigh can do? Why?* This party was epic too. My mind wouldn't stop, and my heart kept crying out to God even though my lips were silent and my feelings were hiding well behind the smile on my face.

Right there in the middle of my pity party, though, I felt the Holy Spirit speak to my heart and say, *"You know she wasn't supposed to even be here running at all."* In that moment, while standing on my deck, I was transported back to our hospital room eight years earlier. I heard the doctors tell us how Liana would never walk—yet here she is running. They said she would never talk—but here she is laughing and talking a million words a minute with her friends. We had dreamed of this day. Prayed for it. Believed for it. Now I was standing in it.

I was living in the middle of my dream but had lost my sense of gratitude.

The miracles I prayed for were staring me in the face and I had gotten used to them. Eight years ago we cried out to God and prayed and begged the Lord to heal the twins. We prayed every day that they would be filled with joy and laughter. And at their eighth birthday party, they were. But I was so consumed with what wasn't happening that I lost sight of what did happen, and what was happening right before my very eyes.

I am convinced more than ever that when we are focused on the one thing we feel God won't give us, we lose sight of the countless miracles we are currently living in. We become numb to the dreams that have been realized all around us.

God is a Father who has given far more than he has withheld. Even what he withholds from us is ultimately for our good.

As I said, this wasn't the only pity party I had attended. In that moment when I heard God telling me, *"This dream is not for you,"* seven years into my time at Elevation, I had a similar party. But I didn't see that I was already standing in the middle of the dream I had prayed for in Nashville almost two decades earlier. I was mourning my current dream while failing to see that God had been faithful to bring an old dream to pass. And this happens more times than I care to admit.

God is at work fulfilling dreams all around us if we just look for his goodness. Unfortunately, I miss the miracles because my mind and heart are prone to forgetfulness. When I forget my prayers and God's presence in my life, I end up not seeing the ways he has orchestrated my life, and I become dissatisfied with my circumstances, even though they are what I prayed for— almost exactly—and what I thought years ago would make me happy.

While I might be grateful at one point, in a moment when I recognize that God has answered a prayer, that sense of gratitude in my heart always seems to leak out. My heart may be full in the morning, but if I'm not careful to guard it, by the end of the day, tiny holes begin to form from the attacks of difficult circumstances and sin. And when that happens, my gratitude leaks faster than I can replenish it.

THE SUMMER OF SURVIVOR

In the summer of 2020, because of the pandemic our family spent all of our time at home. One evening we randomly watched an episode of *Survivor*—season 28, "Cagayan," when Tony so deviously used his spy shack—and we were hooked. A new obsession was born.

We went back to the beginning and spent countless hours making our way from season to season, learning the lessons of alliance building, winning immunity challenges, shelter building, and of course how to do it all with minimal food and water. My twins even wanted a *Survivor* birthday party, at which they betrayed an alliance with their own father to secure victory. It still stings.

If you've watched *Survivor*, you know that as soon as the contestants arrive at their tropical destination, they have to do two things—make a fire and find water. The fire is crucial for a lot of things, chief of which is to boil water so that they don't get sick from drinking it. Usually the teams that find water first and then make a fire to purify the water perform well on the first several challenges, while those who don't quickly become very weak. Without water, they lack the strength or stamina to compete. Water is everything. Without it, you see the strongest contestants lose their strength, motivation, and any semblance of good attitudes. For that reason, when a tribe gets clean water, they guard it like a million dollars, because without water, there is no chance of winning and receiving the reward.

Gratitude is as important to our souls as water is to our bodies. You can go for a little while without gratitude, but it must be replenished if you want to live. It's crucial to our spiritual survival. Gratitude is not optional. With gratitude, we can navigate any challenge that life throws our way. Without it, the worries and burdens of life end up killing us. We stop trusting. We stop hoping. We stop obeying. We stop growing. And we stop moving forward.

When I lose my gratitude, I lose my ability to see reality clearly. At the risk of overusing the water metaphor, let me give you another image. Do you remember the classic image of the wanderer in the desert who is out of water and parched with thirst, only to be repeatedly fooled with a mirage of an oasis? I don't know if that scenario has ever actually happened, but hallucinations are a symptom of severe dehydration. When you don't have enough water in your body, you can't see reality accurately. In exactly the same way, gratitude is essential for us to see a true picture of what God is actually doing around us. With gratitude in your heart, you see more accurately the goodness of God around you. Without it, you fail to see his kindness both in giving gifts and withholding things that are harmful. You see a closed door as punishment when it may be protection. We need the lens of gratitude to give us eyes to see.

At my eight-year-old twins' birthday party, when I didn't have gratitude, all I could see was what I thought God *wasn't* doing instead of what he *was* doing right in front of my eyes.

Could it be that we are living in the fulfillment of more of our dreams than we realize, but we don't appreciate them or maximize them to the fullest because we are blinded by a lack of gratitude?

We must do everything in our power to guard the gratitude in our hearts. To protect it. And to fuel it. When we are standing in the middle of a miracle, one of the most important things we can do is learn to guard our gratitude.

THE ENTITLEMENT TRAP

One of the greatest enemies of gratitude in my life is a sense of entitlement. A sense that I deserve more than I have. I hate to admit it, but I am prone to think that I am entitled to my dream more than someone else is entitled to theirs.

I didn't want to acknowledge that entitlement was in my heart, but the more I peeled back the layers of envy, bitterness, and frustration triggered by setbacks in achieving my dream, I could see that entitlement was underneath, crowding out my gratitude.

In Matthew 20 Jesus gives us his teaching on entitlement:

For the kingdom of heaven is like a landowner who went out early in the morning to hire workers for his vineyard. He agreed to pay them a denarius for the day and sent them into his vineyard.

About nine in the morning he went out and saw others standing in the marketplace doing nothing. He told them, "You also go and work in my vineyard, and I will pay you whatever is right." So they went.

He went out again about noon and about three in the afternoon and did the same thing. About five in the afternoon he went out and found still others standing around. He asked them, "Why have you been standing here all day long doing nothing?"

"Because no one has hired us," they answered.

He said to them, "You also go and work in my vineyard."

When evening came, the owner of the vineyard said to his foreman, "Call the workers and pay them their wages, beginning with the last ones hired and going on to the first."

The workers who were hired about five in the afternoon came and each received a denarius. So when those came who were hired first, they expected to receive more. But each one of them also received a denarius. When they received it, they began to grumble against the landowner. "These who were hired last worked only one hour," they said, "and you have made them equal to us who have borne the burden of the work and the heat of the day."

But he answered one of them, "I am not being unfair to you, friend. Didn't you agree to work for a denarius? Take your pay and go. I want to give the one who was hired last the same as I gave you. Don't I have the right to do what I want with my own money? Or are you envious because I am generous?"

So the last will be first, and the first will be last. (vv. 1–16)

It's hard to not have sympathy for the workers who worked all day. They worked longer hours, probably in the heat of the day and under tougher conditions, than those who joined the job toward the end of the day. On the surface Jesus' lesson doesn't seem fair.

But here is what the passage is saying: The workers who worked all day were at first perfectly happy with their wage. They agreed to it from the beginning. If the late workers weren't there, the early workers would have been entirely satisfied with what they had earned. The problem wasn't with what they had been given. The problem was with what someone else received. The early workers didn't think the latecomers deserved what they got. That was the source of the grumbling.

The early workers grumbled after they saw others being blessed. At that moment, the gratitude they once had for what they had been offered was gone. Their entitlement crowded out their gratitude. The workers who arrived first now believed they deserved more. They thought they were owed something else. What they had been paid, and would have once been satisfied with, was no longer enough. The workers who had labored all day were now envious because the master was generous.

Have you ever been thankful for where you are in life, or the progress you have made toward your dream, until you see someone else who is further along or, even worse, who you think doesn't deserve success to begin with? What does that comparison do to your gratitude? I may not grumble to others, but I have had many massive grumbling sessions in my mind. They go a little something like this: *If they have it, why don't I? They are selfish. They don't treat people well. They haven't paid their dues like me. They don't want other people to succeed like I do.*

The sad truth is, I am content in my race until I look over and see someone else who is further along in theirs. When I stop to grumble about someone else running their race, I stop running my own. I'm now spending my energy grumbling and trying to win a debate against an opponent that's only in my head. I stack up the evidence for why I deserve the opportunity or blessing given to this other person more than they do.

I act just like one of the entitled workers in Matthew 20.

So what are we to do?

First, focus on running your race, and stop wasting energy wishing you were running someone else's.

Second, and most importantly, no matter how much you think someone else doesn't deserve it, the truth is you both don't deserve it. We are all running by the grace of God. None of it is deserved. It is all a gift.

We have all been invited into doing the work of the kingdom of God by a generous Father who didn't have to include us. Yet we are envious because the Master is generous, without realizing the Master has also been generous to us.

Entitlement is uprooted when we truly grasp the depths of God's grace and just how undeserved it is. When we understand this, our grumbling is silenced by gratitude and praise for all the fulfilled dreams that surround us.

I am convinced that in this life, before we see Christ face-to-face, no one human will fully understand the grace of God. But there are disciplines that we can develop to help us shape a heart and a mind capable of understanding God's heart and to help us begin, slowly and daily, to glean more and more of his amazing grace. And as a result, gratitude will abound.

These disciplines are simple. Anyone can do them at any time. They involve simply a shift of focus and attention.

Gratitude isn't a feeling. It's a focus.

THE DISCIPLINE OF DIRECTING MY AWARENESS

Let's return to Matthew 20. When I read the passage, I see myself as a worker who accepted the job early and worked all day. A worker who "deserved" more. But if I look at my life, and if I'm honest, I'm more like one of the workers who barely got in to work before the end of the day. One of the workers who were in the right place at the right time, who made it in by the skin of their teeth. The story of my life has actually been more about the goodness shown to a late arrival.

I would have missed that revelation if I hadn't looked back

at my life as a whole, and seen that where I am today—my priv-
ileges, talents, health, family, friends, and so on—is due to the
grace of God and of others. I tend to live life with blinders on,
seeing only what supports the narrative about my dreams. And
what I see is just a small part of the story. There's a much larger
narrative, if I would just open my eyes. God wants me to be
aware of the much larger, comprehensive story of his goodness
toward me.

Only when I direct my mind and thoughts toward the larger
narrative can I actually see my life in a way that produces gratitude and praise. I must discipline my heart to see my life as God
sees it.

David models for us this kind of awareness. After receiving a
"No" from God, he could have grumbled, saying that he deserved
this honor as king, not Solomon. He could have made a case to
God that Solomon had done nothing to deserve this. He would
have been right, but David didn't deserve to be king either. It was
a gift of God's grace to a shepherd boy. David knew that, so he
chose to see things from God's perspective. We see David direct
his heart away from the no and toward gratitude as he prays:

Then King David went in and sat before the LORD, and
he said:

"Who am I, Sovereign LORD, and what is my family,
that you have brought me this far? And as if this were
not enough in your sight, Sovereign LORD, you have also

spoken about the future of the house of your servant—and this decree, Sovereign LORD, is for a mere human!

"What more can David say to you? For you know your servant, Sovereign LORD. For the sake of your word and according to your will, you have done this great thing and made it known to your servant." (2 Samuel 7:18–21)

In his prayer David reminds himself of what he had been given and how undeserved it was. He directs his awareness not to the house he has been denied building, but instead to the house God has promised him. David may not have felt gratitude in this moment, but he knew when he directed his thoughts to the goodness of God toward him, his emotions and heart would follow.

Like David, we need to look at the whole story, take ourselves out of the chapter we are in, and remember the ones that came before. Sometimes I try to have a conversation with fifteen-year-old Wade, who dreamed about being in ministry like his granddad. I remember teenage Wade, who just started playing guitar and wished he could write a song. Fifteen-year-old Wade would be speechless at what forty-five-year-old Wade's life looks like. He wouldn't be frustrated that other people got more opportunities. He would be blown away that any of this ever happened.

There are small, practical ways to direct your awareness daily to your full story. One way is through journaling. Edgar, one of the incredible worship leaders at Elevation, texted one day thanking me for sending him a direct message on Instagram exactly one year earlier. From that message, a conversation arose that eventually resulted in his coming on staff. After he sent me this text, I asked him how he remembered that specific date, and he said that he had written it down in his five-year journal.

If you aren't familiar with a five-year journal (I wasn't), it's a journal that has a page for each day of the year, and on each page you can write something on that date over the span of five successive years. So in your second year you see your thoughts on that date a year earlier, and on and on for five years. You can recall a conversation of encouragement that you would have normally forgotten. You can celebrate years later a provision God made for you. You can remember a small prayer you prayed that was granted to you. This kind of exercise has the power to fight forgetfulness and help you remember how far God has brought you. Edgar was grateful because he put a discipline into practice that helped him remember.

THE DISCIPLINE OF DIRECTING MY ANTICIPATION

I used to think that I didn't struggle with cynicism. I'm a fairly positive person, and I can even be optimistic to a fault. Recently, though, I caught myself saying to myself something like this: *Well, yes, God did that then, but my best days are behind me. It's all downhill now. My dream could never actually happen. I'm too old. I've had my chance. I blew it. Why would God want to bless me?*

These kinds of indictments occur in my thoughts more often than I'm aware, I'm sure. But what's more troubling is that underneath this cynicism is the belief that the goodness and grace of God have a limit. That God's grace was enough to save me, but not enough to sustain me on a daily basis. I act as if I get only a limited amount of his grace, and that I've used it all up in the past and don't have any left for my present moment. I live as if grace may have saved me then, but now I have to work to earn God's approval.

As I chase my dreams, deep down I've been trying this whole time to prove to God that I'm worthy of being blessed, which ends always in defeat because I know myself and how unworthy I actually am.

To clear my head during the day, I like to get out of the office and take walks. I put my AirPods in so people think I'm listening to a podcast or on a call, but I just want to be silent and hear from God. (I guess my secret's out now—it was good while it lasted.) During one of these walks, I was wrestling with feelings of not being where I wanted to be in life. My dreams were coming up short. As I brought my heart to God, I sensed him respond by saying, *"Do you realize that if you didn't do anything at all for me, you are just as valuable to me as my child?"* I wanted to say, *"Yes, Lord. Of course I know that,"* but I knew my actions and thoughts proved that I didn't. I was cynical that God's grace had limits, and I had a hard time believing that I mattered to Jesus apart from my ministry résumé. I couldn't fully accept that I didn't have to earn God's approval.

David writes in Psalm 103,

Let all that I am praise the LORD;
may I never forget the good things he does for me.
(v. 2 NLT)

If you read the verse quickly, you probably thought that the good things it refers to are in the past. Read it again. While certainly the verse is referring to things God has done in the past, the tense there is present: "May I never forget the good things he does for me."

God's goodness is in the present tense. I am not just grateful for what he did in the past. I am looking for his goodness in the present. This means we can live with what Peter describes as "great expectation." Not cynicism that things won't work out, but with anticipation that God is working on something beautiful.

You sense that anticipation in David's prayer after Nathan delivers the message about the temple:

And now, LORD God, keep forever the promise you have made concerning your servant and his house. Do as you promised, so that your name will be great forever. Then people will say, "The LORD Almighty is God over Israel!" And the house of your servant David will be established in your sight.

LORD Almighty, God of Israel, you have revealed this to your servant, saying, "I will build a house for you." So your servant has found courage to pray this prayer to you.

Sovereign Lord, you are God! Your covenant is trust-worthy, and you have promised these good things to your servant. Now be pleased to bless the house of your servant, that it may continue forever in your sight; for you, Sovereign Lord, have spoken, and with your blessing the house of your servant will be blessed forever. (2 Samuel 7:25–29)

David saw God's goodness and it gave him courage to believe that God was working even in the setback of his dream. David anticipated God's fulfillment of his promise. David anticipated God's blessing.

I want to be on the lookout for blessings, because if I truly look, they are everywhere. Blessings are found in victory and defeat.

Instead of wishing you were in a different season, or someone else's season, find the blessing in this season.

One helpful and simple way we can practice this discipline is by saying the Lord's Prayer daily.

At lunch every day I get an alert on my watch or phone telling me to pray. Most days, no matter where I'm at, I pray the Lord's Prayer. Depending on where I am, I may have to say it to myself or under my breath, but regardless, I take the time to re-center myself on Christ and his kingdom. Because the prayer was Jesus' prayer, it serves to ground me in what was important to Jesus. And because the prayer was one of the first Christian creeds, when I pray it, my heart is aligning with the mission of the kingdom of God. Saying the Lord's Prayer helps me to look for the kingdom at work, and how God is inviting me into it.

THE DISCIPLINE OF DIRECTING MY APPLAUSE

Most of my entitlement comes from obsessive self-absorption. My operating system says that all of God's plans and purposes in the world have me at the center. This is my default, unfortunately. And so to break away from this pattern of thinking, I need something to shock the system, and the best way I have found to do this is to become the champion of someone else—especially someone who is doing what I wish I could do. This is like the greatest judo move on the devil. Using something he thought would take you out to actually make you more grateful.

Jesus ends this parable of the workers with one of the great truths of the kingdom: "So the last will be first, and the first will be last" (Matt. 20:16).

In fact, he revisits this idea later in the same chapter when the mother of James and John asks Jesus if her sons can sit on his right and left in the kingdom of God. Jesus in a patient but firm way explains the error of her motive behind the question:

"You don't know what you are asking," Jesus said to them. "Can you drink the cup I am going to drink?"

"We can," they answered.

Jesus said to them, "You will indeed drink from my cup, but to sit at my right or left is not for me to grant. These places belong to those for whom they have been prepared by my Father."

When the ten heard about this, they were indignant with the two brothers. Jesus called them together and said, "You know that the rulers of the Gentiles lord it over them, and their high officials exercise authority over them. Not so with you. Instead, whoever wants to become great among you must be your servant, and whoever wants to be first must be your slave—just as the Son of Man did not come to be served, but to serve, and to give his life as a ransom for many." (Matthew 20:22–28)

Jesus clearly states that there is a different power structure in the kingdom of God. Rulers lead through serving, not by brandishing their power or ambition. As one of my friends likes to say, the path to greatness isn't through status, but through service.

I have struggled with what this looks like in real life. Am I always supposed to make myself last? That seems to go against bringing my best effort and passion to what I work toward. But I don't think Jesus is telling us not to work hard, compete, or get ahead.

His teaching here rests on the foundation that any place of prominence is for the Father to give. You can take heart in the fact that your dream or promotion is not held in the hands of man, but instead in the hands of your Father.

If I trust God enough with my dream, my future, and my promotion in life, I am then free to help someone else walk in their dream. Instead of trying to make myself last, I help push someone else to the front. I use my position and influence to actively serve and help others. I discipline myself to direct my applause to someone else. I don't have to fight for or protect my spot. Instead, I believe that God wants to use my service in the life of someone else to help bring their dream to pass. That is the way the kingdom works.

I have found that a deeper sense of gratitude wells up within me when I know God has used me to help someone else. When I step outside of myself and serve someone else in their dream.

Be the biggest source of applause in someone else's life. Nothing could be a greater display of the gospel or kingdom of God than actively seeking to help someone else get an opportunity or blessing that you want.

Here again David models this well:

> David also said to Solomon his son, "Be strong and courageous, and do the work. Do not be afraid or discouraged, for the Lord God, my God, is with you. He will not fail you or forsake you until all the work for the service of the temple of the Lord is finished. The divisions of the priests and Levites are ready for all the work on the temple of God, and every willing person skilled in any craft will help you in all the work. The officials and all the people will obey your every command." (1 Chronicles 28:20–21)

David humbles himself, setting up for success the person who will live David's dream. And he not only encourages his son Solomon but he also offers material support. Are we willing to do this, or do we secretly wish failure on others to show how undeserving they are of the dream?

One of the most powerful things Pastor Steven said to me was "Mature ministry is being more excited about what God does through others than what he does through you."

When you pivot from thinking life revolves around you to being an advocate of someone else's dream, you join in the mission of something infinitely greater—the kingdom of God.

Discipline the direction of your heart. Direct it toward the right awareness of what God is doing. Direct it toward anticipating good from the Lord. Direct your applause to be a champion of others. When you do these things, and make it a constant practice, you will find a new appreciation for the grace of God in your life. And where grace abounds, gratitude is always present.

PIVOT PRACTICE

- Which discipline of direction do you need to put into practice the most? How can you direct your awareness, anticipation, and applause toward what fuels your faith, rather than toward what is fighting against it?
- What daily disciplines can you put in place that will tangibly impact the health of your gratitude?

Reawaken Your Expectation and Keep Dreaming

I write this final chapter on the evening of my forty-fifth birth-day. It hasn't been hard to pivot today, because God's goodness has been overwhelmingly evident to me as I reflect on my life up to this point.

There were times I doubted I would feel this way. I think back to the conversation many years earlier when I first heard *"This dream is not for you."* That conversation took place roughly seven years into my time at Elevation. For seven years I got to live my dream. During that time I cherished how good God had been to me, and from those years I saw a clear picture of what

I would miss out on if I laid my dream down. I saw that other people would take on my role at Elevation and live my dream in my place. One voice in my heart told me God was trustworthy. Another voice told me my best was behind me now. At every turn, faith and fear have always been there side by side, telling me very different stories.

I didn't know if I could live a life of joy or purpose without my dream. Yet here I am, close to ten years after that conversation and the death of my dream. I've spent more time without that dream—Wade the worship leader, Wade the songwriter, Wade a part of Elevation Worship—than I did living it. I'm here to testify: There is life after your dream has died. That might sound a bit dramatic, but oftentimes we act as if we can't live without our dreams.

It's nearly a decade after the death of my dream, and I can truly say that I love Jesus more than I ever have in my life. I have experienced his grace, faithfulness, and kindness in a more tangible way than ever. He has been so good to me.

None of this is my own doing. I wish I could say I settled the matter in my heart all those years ago. Believe me, I have made numerous attempts to go my own way. But the Holy Spirit has been transforming my heart—through pruning. What you have read in this book are just a few of the lessons I have learned.

There have been several key moments in this journey when these lessons have been clearer than others. Times when I wasn't entering class eager to learn, but when the voice of God's Spirit still spoke in his mercy and grace toward me. One such time when

I was feeling particularly aimless, when I didn't quite see the fruit of trusting God, was in 2016. I had been walking through this process of letting my dream die for a couple of years. In fact, it's not an exaggeration to say that I was in the middle of a spiritual identity crisis, not knowing who I was anymore or what use I was to God without the role I had previously known. I was right in the middle of redefining my life not by a dream, but by something greater. It was messy and it hurt.

On December 3, 2016, I hit a low point. I was praying in my room on a Saturday morning asking God if he even saw me anymore. Did he notice what I was going through or feeling? I was trying my best to trust him. I was trying to be faithful and do what I thought was right, but the circumstances were especially difficult. I wasn't seeing the joy or peace that I thought followed obedience. In fact, I was tempted to abandon ministry altogether. Even worse, I was tempted to give up on trusting God. My prayers consisted of this all-too-familiar question on repeat: *Did I miss it?*

At that precise moment, as I was crying out to God, my mom sent me a text with two screenshots of a devotional she had seen online earlier that day. It was written by Wendy Alsup, with whom I was unfamiliar at that time. What made the text even more unexpected was that I hadn't told my mom I was wrestling with any of this. I tend to not want people to know I am struggling, and so I kept private the battle going on in my heart. I don't recommend that as a healthy approach, but that's where I was then.

The two screenshots my mom sent weren't even the whole devotional. They were just two random parts from the middle of the devotional without context. But these two screenshots were all I needed, because the following words gripped my heart immediately:

> Dear friend struggling with a weight on your shoulders, one that may seem lighter to bear if you just walked away from God's instructions: Don't buy that lie. It was the first lie ever told, and it remains Satan's great summary temptation: "God's instructions are a limitation. They will keep you from all you're meant to be."
>
> No, it's not true. Embrace the path of suffering in obedience to God's instructions. Lose your life. Let go of yourself and your life. Let go of yourself and your expectations. And trust God to meet you, redeem your story, and give you a place of import in his larger story. As you lose your right to your story, you emerge in a much greater one, and what you will find is *worth it*.
>
> I've walked a hard path, and I continue to walk a hard path. But God gave me manna to sustain me at the hardest points and had blessed me abundantly even through the removal of things I thought I couldn't live without. He has proven himself to me, and he has proven to me the goodness of his words. When others tried to encourage me by telling me I wasn't constrained by God's instructions,

I found instead abundant grace and help when I felt convicted that I was.

It requires faith to stay in that process. I cannot produce such faith in you. You cannot produce it in yourself. But you can lean into the One who can.

May you one day look back in praise of the God who turns stones into bread, water into wine, and loss into life abundant. (Wendy Alsup[1])

When I read this, at that moment, God spoke louder than any audible voice. His word was clear and unmistakable. He was reassuring me, not as an ex–worship leader trying to find his way, but as a beloved son in need of the reassurance of his Father. He was telling me:

"You didn't miss it, because you can never lose when you give me everything you have. Don't give up on trusting me. I am calling you into a greater story than you could ever write on your own. And this chapter will not define the story."

God is writing a larger story, and he was inviting me to participate in that story, if I would just let go and surrender. He was reminding me that every ounce of trust would be worth it.

Up until that moment, I had thought that letting go meant

---

1   Wendy Alsup, "Dying to Self in the Age of Self-Love," TGC, emphasis in original, https://www.thegospelcoalition.org/article/dying-to-self-in-the-age-of-self-love/.

giving up on my dream, or giving up the right to dream again. But I was wrong. Letting go is not the same as giving up.

Yes, I must let go of the right to my story, at least in the way I want to tell it. But in the process of giving up my rights, and letting go of control of my life, I started to open myself up to a much greater story—and greater purpose—that eclipsed anything I could have ever dreamed. I was opening myself up to new dreams. Greater dreams. The Father's dreams.

What the Lord told me then, I want to tell you now.

Don't give up. Don't stop dreaming. Don't stop trusting God even though life looks different than you expected.

David didn't stop dreaming when God told him no. If anything, he began to dream bigger. He started dreaming of the impact through legacy. He saw generations and generations blessed by what God had promised through a new dream. David didn't give up. He surrendered and worked toward something greater.

In his wildest dreams, I don't think David could ever have grasped where his trust would lead. This man after God's own heart who, while not perfect, truly sought to let go and trust God, was the man God used to establish a house that would one day bring forth humanity's redemption through the Messiah. His trust helped pave the way for Jesus.

God saw past the four walls David wanted to construct to house the Spirit of the Lord. God saw the ultimate dwelling place of his Spirit within the hearts of his people. He was up to something greater, something mysterious, and he invited David into that. David didn't know what was on the other side of his obedience and surrender. Nor would he see it in his lifetime. But he didn't give up or stop trusting in the goodness and purpose of God. He kept dreaming although he never lived in the reality of what was promised. He was looking ahead to something greater than immediate gratification. On this side of the cross and resurrection, I believe David would say that letting his dream die was worth it.

So that Saturday morning in December after reading the devotional my mom sent, I decided I couldn't give up. I wanted to let go of my need to direct my own life, and fully surrender to the control and direction of Christ. This was a process, and even today remains a decision I must remake every day, often many times a day. But on that Saturday morning, I put a stake in the ground. That was my true moment of surrender.

I can tell you now with confidence and awe that I have never regretted that decision to trust God. I'm living in the reality of dreams I once prayed, fasted, and worked for. My daughters are healthy and thriving, and I continue to be amazed at the fruit of the ministry at Elevation Church. Songs that I was blessed to help write, and even more that I didn't write, have encouraged the church around the world. God has been so good.

I've also mourned dreams that have died. There's been no resurrection of my dream to be a worship leader and songwriter. I've left the staff at Elevation Church and transitioned away from the worship ministry the Lord allowed me to have a hand in building. Yet God continues to be good. Other people at Elevation are accomplishing the things I prayed and worked for.

I've also started to dream new dreams. Dreams for my family. Dreams for my children. Dreams for the church. Dreams of how I can be a father and mentor to others in ministry. And new dreams of how I can steward, Lord willing, the next forty-five years of my life, declaring the goodness of God to those who will listen. Writing this book is one of those new dreams. I can't limit God to doing incredible things in only the first half of my life. That's just the foundation. And no matter what happens with any of my dreams, I know that God is always and forever good.

Whether you are living in a dream, burying one that has died, or birthing a new dream, I am here to testify to one simple truth: Jesus can be trusted.

He can be trusted with your dream, yes. But more importantly, he can be trusted with your heart. That's what he wants more than anything. The process of surrendering our hearts and our lives is painful at times, but it is worth it. There is no dream that is greater than truly knowing Jesus. Knowing him as Lord, yet also knowing him as a friend.

So don't give up on dreaming, but more importantly, don't give up on trusting Jesus. Release whatever he calls you to release. Go wherever he calls you to go. Stay wherever he calls you to stay. And be the kind of person our heavenly Father is calling all of us to be as his sons and daughters.

And as you live this life of trust, you are not resigning yourself to a dreamless life. If anything, you are opening yourself to the surprises God will bring into your life—things that you could have never expected. Live openhanded, anticipating that he will bring dreams to pass. You'll be amazed at the way he brings new life and expression to a dream you thought was dead years ago, and you'll see that he wanted to bring it to life all along. Be open to dreaming a dream that hasn't even crossed your mind. And be ready for God to surprise you with the revelation that you can live a life of joy and purpose even if you don't get anything you dreamed of—because in Christ you already have all that your soul needs.

This dream is not for you.

But there is something so much greater. So much bigger than you. And you will find that it is worth it. Every dream laid down for Christ will be resurrected into something far more beautiful and valuable in his kingdom.

ACKNOWLEDGMENTS

This book is the story of God's faithfulness in my life, and so much of his goodness has been expressed through the people who not only have walked this journey with me, but who have also encouraged me every step of the way to share it with you.

Ferris, you are the daily evidence of Ephesians 3:20–21 in my life, for you are truly more than I could have asked for or imagined. Thank you for dreaming with me in the seasons that seemed full of possibility, and in the darkest moments when dreaming only seemed to lead to disappointment. Through it all, God has spoken to me the most time and time again through you. I love you.

Liana, Adleigh, and Sydney, you fill our home with joy and laughter and are the delight of my life. This story is your story, too, and each of you are a testimony of the miracle-working power of Jesus. It's my greatest joy to watch you not only dream your own dreams, but to see you place those dreams in the hands of your Father in heaven. Each of you have a relationship with God that inspires me more than you know. I can't wait for the day that people are reading the words that come from your pen (or iPad). That is when they will realize that I am the least talented writer in the Joye family.

Acknowledgments

Mom and Dad, no one has championed what God has put in me, or encouraged me to trust Christ, more than you have. Thank you for not just telling me about Jesus, but leading me to him and showing me what it means to walk with him. The lessons I share in this book were built on the foundation of faith that you laid for me. These words might have come from my heart, but you planted the seeds that produced them.

Thank you to Ryan Peterson and the incredible team at Worthy Publishing and Hachette Nashville for not only believing in this message, but for also believing in me and taking a chance on a first time author. Ryan, it has especially been a joy to work with you through the editing process. Thank you for your grace and patience as you shared your experience and wisdom with me.

Thank you to Trinity McFadden and Alexander Field and the team at The Bindery for continuing to work with me and championing this book even when I walked away mid-process from a very large platform. Your trust that this was a book people needed gave me the faith to believe it myself.

Pastor Steven, thank you for taking a chance on me in 2007 and giving me the privilege of helping build a church that God has used to change my life. The Holy Spirit uses your sermons and songs to speak to people all over the world, as he does in my life, but it's the phone calls you made to me in hospital rooms and the hard but compassionate challenges in meetings when you told me hard things I needed to hear that have proven to be your most pivotal words in my story. Those are the moments when I learned to open my hands and trust Jesus like never before. Thank you for the investment you made in my life that continues to bear fruit through the pages of this book.

Chunks, thank you for being a great leader, advocate, and friend who has gone above and beyond to help me live my dreams—both when I was on staff, and even now in this new journey.

Stephen Brewster, thank you for making the connection with The Bindery and for always speaking so much belief in me over the years. I'm extremely grateful for your friendship and how you model mature ministry by being more excited about what God does through others than what he does through you.

Chris Brown, while it was an honor to serve with you on staff for fourteen years building Elevation, it's an even greater honor to call you a brother and friend. Thank you for always being a voice of encouragement in the seasons of transition when I doubted what God had put in me. You were one of the first people to read these words and your enthusiasm about them made me believe there might be something to this book idea. Ferris and I love you and your family so much.

Larry Hubatka, it's one of God's kindest gifts in this new season to renew our friendship and for Ferris and I to walk closely alongside you and Kelly like we did for many years at Elevation. Thank you for giving me greater courage to pursue releasing a book I had written that no one knew about yet. I'm glad I did. JRS.

Stephen Webb, thank you for taking the time that weekend

in June of 2021 to send me voice memo after voice memo after you read the first draft of this manuscript. You went above and beyond to help me, and I'll always be grateful for the way you seek to push others forward. I am better, and this book is as well, because of it.

Reggi Beasley, thank you for reading an early version of the book and for always giving me thoughtful and needed insight.

Brian Schindler, thank you for helping me build so many crucial aspects of the work God has called me to this year. Knowing you were on the team allowed me to confidently give my focus on finishing this manuscript.

Graham Cochrane, I love how God has brought our paths together over the last year. Your coaching has helped push me to confidently carry this message with a bold humility, believing it is necessary in this generation and therefore I can't back down in sharing it with conviction.

Mark Maxwell, thank you for all your guidance in finalizing the partnership that allows this message to go out to the people who need it.

Carlos Whittaker, you had me teary eyed on a plane headed home from Texas as I read the foreword you wrote. I am so grateful for your words, and for the kindness your family demonstrated to ours as we stepped into an exciting but scary season at the beginning of 2022.

Lee McDerment, years ago I got a text from you telling me about a dream you had about how I was going to write a book that would help a lot of people, especially worship leaders. What you didn't know was I had secretly been dreaming about this book but had only told me wife about it. Thank you for confirming a dream that God had put it me when it was incubating in silence. It was the first step on the road that has led me here.

Lauren Anderson, the email you sent to me in September of 2020 with the prophetic word that it was time to release what God had put in me came the exact morning I was praying and asking God if I should write this book. Thank you for your obedience and allowing the Lord to speak through you.

Most importantly, thank you, Jesus. You are the source of every good and perfect gift in my life. This book tells just a fraction of the story of your goodness towards me.

Wade Joye is a speaker, Bible teacher, ministry coach, and host of the Dreamers & Disciples podcast. Prior to beginning his current ministry, he was the worship pastor at Elevation Church in Charlotte, North Carolina, for fourteen years. During that time, Wade not only led worship on the main stage but he also wrote and recorded original worship songs, preached, and toured. Wade and his wife, Ferris, have three daughters they adore, and are learning to navigate family, ministry, and faith as they raise children with special needs.